Written Solutions for Odd Numbered Exercise Problems To
Mathematics for Business
4th Edition*

Natalie Yang

*by Gary Bronson
Richard Bronson
Maureen Kieff
Natalie Yang

ACKNOWLEDGMENT

I would like to thank Dr. Gary Bronson, Dr. Richard Bronson, Professor Kieff and the DSCI Department Chair, Dr. Wang, for their support in this endeavor.

DEDICATION

To Hong, Rachel, Benjamin, and My Parents

<u>NOTES</u>

1. Excel is a registered trademark of Microsoft Corporation.

2. Every effort has been made to make this solution manual as accurate as possible. No warranty of suitability, purpose, or fitness is implied, and the information is provided on an as is basis. The author assumes no liability or responsibility to any person or entity with respect to loss or damage from the use of the information contained in this manual.

3. There may be a small discrepancy between the answers in this manual and the Excel spreadsheet output because the spreadsheet internal calculations use higher precision.

Table of Contents

Chapter 1 The Basics: A Review

Section 1.1: Signed Numbers

1. $3 + (-6) = -3$

3. $19.7 + (-18.1) = 1.6$

5. $-9 + \left(-\frac{1}{2}\right) = -\left(9 + \frac{1}{2}\right) = -9\frac{1}{2} = -\frac{19}{2}$

7. $9(18) = 162$

9. $(-9)(18) = -(9 \cdot 18) = -162$

11. $(2)\left(-\frac{1}{3}\right) = -\left(2 \cdot \frac{1}{3}\right) = -\left(\frac{2}{1} \cdot \frac{1}{3}\right) = -\frac{2}{3}$

13. $(-6.1)(2.3) = -(6.1 \cdot 2.3) = -14.03$

15. $\frac{(-8)}{(-2)} = \frac{8}{2} = 4$

17. $\frac{-8}{2} = -\frac{8}{2} = -4$

19. $\frac{4}{-5} = -\frac{4}{5}$

21. $\frac{-22}{4} = -\frac{2 \cdot 11}{2 \cdot 2} = -\frac{11}{2} = -5.5$

23. $4 - 8 = 4 + (-8) = -4$

25. $-4 - (-8) = -4 + 8 = 4$

27. $-8 - (-4) = (-8) + 4 = -4$

29. $-5.6 - 2.1 = (-5.6) + (-2.1) = -7.7$

31. $2[5 + (-3)] = 2[2] = 2 \cdot 2 = 4$

33. $-4(1 - 3) + 2(2 - 5) = -4(-2) + 2(-3) = 8 + (-6) = 2$

35. $(1.6)(1.9 - 2.1) - 6.3 = (1.6)(-0.2) - 6.3 = -0.32 - 6.3 = (-0.32) + (-6.3) = -6.62$

37. $\frac{8[1-(-8)]-2[7-1]}{2} = \frac{8[1+8]-2[6]}{2} = \frac{8[9]-2[6]}{2} = \frac{8 \cdot 9 - 2 \cdot 6}{2} = \frac{72-12}{2} = \frac{60}{2} = 30$

39. $\frac{(5-11)(8-14)+42(2+3)}{7[2(1+30)-3(2-5)]} = \frac{(-6)(-6)+42(5)}{7[2(31)-3(-3)]} = \frac{36+210}{7[62+9]} = \frac{246}{7[71]} = \frac{246}{497}$

Section 1.2: Solving Equations Having One Unknown

1. $x = -1$ is a solution to $2x + 3 = 1$ if it satisfies the given equation. Substituting $x = -1$ into the equation, we have: $2(-1) + 3 = -2 + 3 = 1$. Since $x = -1$ satisfied the equation, it is a solution.

3. $p = 1$ is a solution to $2(p + 7) = 3p + 4$ if it satisfies the given equation. Substituting $p = 1$ into the equation, we have:

   Left side of the equation: $2(1 + 7) = 2(8) = 16$

   Right side of the equation: $3(1) + 4 = 3 + 4 = 7$

   Since the left and right sides of the equation do not equal, $p = 1$ is not a solution.

5. $s = 1$ is a solution to $\dfrac{(s+3)(s-2)}{2s+1} = s + 7$ if it satisfies the given equation. Substituting $s = 1$ into the equation, we have:

Left side of the equation: $\dfrac{(s+3)(s-2)}{2s+1} = \dfrac{(1+3)(1-2)}{2(1)+1} = \dfrac{(4)(-1)}{2+1} = \dfrac{-4}{3} = -\dfrac{4}{3}$

Right side of the equation: $s + 7 = 1 + 7 = 8$

Since the left and right sides of the equation do not equal, $s = 1$ is not a solution.

7. $x = 1$ is a solution to $\dfrac{x(y-1)+yz}{y(x-z)} = \dfrac{x}{y}$ if it satisfies the given equation. Substituting $x = 1$ into the equation, we have:

Left side of the equation: $\dfrac{1(2-1)+2(0)}{2(1-0)} = \dfrac{1(1)+0}{2(1)} = \dfrac{1}{2}$

Right side of the equation: $\dfrac{x}{y} = \dfrac{1}{2}$.

Since the left and right sides of the equation are equal, $x = 1$ is a solution.

9. $\begin{aligned} 7 &= 2 + x \\ -2 \quad &\; -2 \\ 5 &= x \quad or \quad x = 5 \end{aligned}$

11. $8x = -16$
$\dfrac{8x}{8} = \dfrac{-16}{8}$
$x = -2$

13. $-4p = 16$
$\dfrac{-4p}{-4} = \dfrac{16}{-4}$
$p = -4$

15. $\begin{aligned} t - 10 &= 4 - t \\ +t \qquad\quad &\quad + t \\ 2t - 10 &= \; 4 \\ +10 \quad &\; + 10 \\ 2t &= 14 \\ \dfrac{2t}{2} &= \dfrac{14}{2} \\ t &= 7 \end{aligned}$

17. $\begin{aligned} 2x &= 3(x + 1) \\ 2x &= 3x + 3 \\ -3x \quad &\; - 3x \\ -1x &= 3 \\ \dfrac{-1x}{-1} &= \dfrac{3}{-1} \\ x &= -3 \end{aligned}$

19. $8(p - 2) = 7(2p + 1)$

$8p - 16 = 14p + 7$

$-14p - 14p$

${-6p} - 16 = 7$

$+16 \quad +16$

$-6p = 23$

$\dfrac{-6p}{-6} = \dfrac{23}{-6}$

$p = -\dfrac{23}{6}$

21. $2(a + 7) - 4 = 3(a - 1) + 2a$

$2a + 14 - 4 = 3a - 3 + 2a$

$2a + 10 = 5a - 3$

$-5a - 5a$

$-3a + 10 = -3$

$-10 \quad - 10$

$-3a = -13$

$\dfrac{-3a}{-3} = \dfrac{-13}{-3}$

$a = \dfrac{-13}{-3} = \dfrac{13}{3}$

23. $\dfrac{2(y-1)+4}{y} = 8$

$y \cdot \left[\dfrac{2(y-1)+4}{y} \right] = 8 \cdot y$

$\cancel{y} \cdot \left[\dfrac{2(y-1)+4}{\cancel{y}} \right] = = 8 \cdot y$

$2(y - 1) + 4 = 8y$

$2y - 2 + 4 = 8y$

$-2y - 2y$

$2 = 6y$

$\dfrac{2}{6} = \dfrac{6y}{6}$ or $\dfrac{6y}{6} = \dfrac{2}{6}$

$y = \dfrac{2}{6} = \dfrac{1}{3}$

25. $\dfrac{3(2t-6)+4(t-8)}{7(6+t)-8(t-4)} = -3$

$\dfrac{6t-18+4t-32}{42+7t-8t+32} = -3$

$\dfrac{10t-50}{-t+74} = -3$

$(-t + 74) \cdot \left[\dfrac{10t-50}{-t+74} \right] = -3 \cdot (-t + 74)$

$\cancel{(-t+74)} \cdot \left[\dfrac{10t-50}{\cancel{-t+74}} \right] = -3 \cdot (-t + 74)$

$10t - 50 = 3t - 222$

$-3t - 3t$

$7t - 50 = -222$

$+50 \quad + 50$

$7t = -172$

$\dfrac{7t}{7} = \dfrac{-172}{7}$

$t = -\dfrac{172}{7}$

Section 1.3: Exponents

1. $\dfrac{3^5 3^4}{3^2 3^3} = \dfrac{3^{5+4}}{3^{2+3}} = \dfrac{3^9}{3^5} = 3^{9-5} = 3^4 = 81$

3. $\dfrac{\pi^4 \left(\pi^2\right)^3}{(\pi^{-2})^4 \pi^3} = \dfrac{\pi^4 \pi^6}{\pi^{-8} \pi^3} = \dfrac{\pi^{4+6}}{\pi^{-8+3}} = \dfrac{\pi^{10}}{\pi^{-5}} = \pi^{10-(-5)} = \pi^{10+5} = \pi^{15}$

5. $\dfrac{(1.7)^{8.1}(1.7)^{-3.4}}{(1.7)^{-4.1}(1.7)^{3.7}} = \dfrac{(1.7)^{8.1+(-3.4)}}{(1.7)^{-4.1+3.7}} = \dfrac{(1.7)^{4.7}}{(1.7)^{-0.4}} = (1.7)^{4.7-(-0.4)} = (1.7)^{4.7+0.4} = (1.7)^{5.1}$

7. $\dfrac{\left(y^{-3}\right)^{-2} y^4 y^{-1}}{y^2 (y^3)^{-1}} = \dfrac{y^6 y^4 y^{-1}}{y^2 y^{-3}} = \dfrac{y^{6+4+(-1)}}{y^{2+(-3)}} = \dfrac{y^9}{y^{-1}} = y^{9-(-1)} = y^{9+1} = y^{10}$

9. $\left\{\left[(3.1)^{-2}\right]^{-4}\right\}^3 = \left\{\left[(3.1)^{(-2)(-4)}\right]\right\}^3 = \left\{\left[(3.1)^8\right]\right\}^3 = (3.1)^{8\cdot3} = (3.1)^{24}$

11. $16^{-5/4} = \left(2^4\right)^{-\frac{5}{4}} = 2^{4\cdot\left(-\frac{5}{4}\right)} = 2^{-\frac{20}{4}} = 2^{-5} = \dfrac{1}{2^5} = \dfrac{1}{32}$

13. $100^{-3/2} = \left(10^2\right)^{-\frac{3}{2}} = 10^{2\cdot\left(-\frac{3}{2}\right)} = 10^{-\frac{6}{2}} = 10^{-3} = \dfrac{1}{10^3} = \dfrac{1}{1000}$

15. $\left(3^{1/3}\right)\left(9^{1/3}\right) = 3^{\frac{1}{3}}(3^2)^{\frac{1}{3}} = 3^{\frac{1}{3}} 3^{2\cdot\frac{1}{3}} = 3^{\frac{1}{3}} 3^{\frac{2}{3}} = 3^{\frac{1}{3}+\frac{2}{3}} = 3^{\frac{3}{3}} = 3^1 = 3$

17. $\left(2^{-3/2}\right)\left(32^{-3/2}\right) = 2^{-\frac{3}{2}}\left(2^5\right)^{-\frac{3}{2}} = 2^{-\frac{3}{2}} 2^{5\cdot\left(-\frac{3}{2}\right)} = 2^{-\frac{3}{2}} 2^{-\frac{15}{2}} = 2^{-\frac{3}{2}+\left(-\frac{15}{2}\right)} = 2^{-\frac{18}{2}}$

$= 2^{-9} = \dfrac{1}{2^9} = \dfrac{1}{512}$

19. $\sqrt{\dfrac{8}{18}} = \sqrt{\dfrac{4\cdot2}{9\cdot2}} = \sqrt{\dfrac{4\cdot\cancel{2}}{9\cdot\cancel{2}}} = \sqrt{\dfrac{4}{9}} = \dfrac{\sqrt{4}}{\sqrt{9}} = \dfrac{2}{3}$

21. $\sqrt[3]{\dfrac{(27)(8)}{125}} = \sqrt[3]{\dfrac{216}{125}} = \dfrac{\sqrt[3]{216}}{\sqrt[3]{125}} = \dfrac{6}{5}$

Section 1.4: Solving Quadratic Equations Using the Quadratic Formula

1. $x^3 = 8$

   $(x^3)^{1/3} = 8^{1/3}$

   $x^{3 \cdot \frac{1}{3}} = \sqrt[3]{8}$

   $x^{\frac{3}{3}} = 2$

   $x = 2$

3. $y^4 = 81$

   $(y^4)^{1/4} = \pm 81^{1/4}$

   $(y^4)^{1/4} = \pm \sqrt[4]{81}$

   $y^{4 \cdot \frac{1}{4}} = \pm 3$

   $y^{\frac{4}{4}} = \pm 3$

   $y = \pm 3$

5. $b^{-2} = \frac{1}{4}$

   $(b^{-2})^{-1/2} = \pm \left(\frac{1}{4}\right)^{-1/2}$

   $(b^{-2})^{-1/2} = \pm (4^{-1})^{-1/2}$

   $b^{(-2) \cdot \left(-\frac{1}{2}\right)} = \pm 4^{1/2}$

   $b^{\frac{2}{2}} = \pm \sqrt{4}$

   $b = \pm 2$

7. $p^5 = 1.3$

   $(p^5)^{1/5} = (1.3)^{1/5}$

   $p^{5\left(\frac{1}{5}\right)} = (1.3)^{1/5}$

   $p = 1.3^{1/5}$

9. $t^{9.3} = 9.3$

   $(t^{9.3})^{1/9.3} = 9.3^{1/9.3}$

   $t^{9.3/9.3} = 9.3^{1/9.3}$

   $t = 9.3^{1/9.3}$

11. **Method 1: Solve by factoring.**

    $(x - 3)(x - 2) = 0$

    $x - 3 = 0 \quad or \quad x - 2 = 0$
    $\quad + 3 \quad +3 \qquad\qquad +2 \quad +2$

    $x = 3 \quad or \quad x = 2$

    Method 2: Solve by the use of the Quadratic Formula.

    $x^2 - 5x + 6 = 0$, where $a = 1, b = -5$, and $c = 6$.

    $$x = \frac{-b \pm \sqrt{b^2 - 4ac}}{2a} = \frac{-(-5) \pm \sqrt{(-5)^2 - 4(1)(6)}}{2(1)} = \frac{5 \pm \sqrt{25 - 24}}{2} = \frac{5 \pm \sqrt{1}}{2} = \frac{5 \pm 1}{2}$$

    $$x_1 = \frac{5 + 1}{2} = \frac{6}{2} = 3 \quad or \quad x_2 = \frac{5 - 1}{2} = \frac{4}{2} = 2$$

13. $2p^2 + 6p - 4 = 0$, where $a = 2, b = 6$, and $c = -4$.

$$p = \frac{-b \pm \sqrt{b^2 - 4ac}}{2a} = \frac{-6 \pm \sqrt{(6)^2 - 4(2)(-4)}}{2(2)} = \frac{-6 \pm \sqrt{36 + 32}}{4} = \frac{-6 \pm \sqrt{68}}{4} = \frac{-6 \pm \sqrt{4 \cdot 17}}{4}$$

$$= \frac{-6 \pm 2\sqrt{17}}{4} = \frac{2(-3 \pm \sqrt{17})}{4} = \frac{-3 \pm \sqrt{17}}{2}$$

$$p_1 = \frac{-3 + \sqrt{17}}{2} \quad \text{or} \quad p_2 = \frac{-3 - \sqrt{17}}{2}$$

15. **Method 1: Solve by factoring.**

$(x + 3)(x + 3) = 0$

$x + 3 = 0$

$\quad -3 \quad -3$

$x = -3$

Method 2: Solve by the use of the Quadratic Formula.

$x^2 + 6x + 9 = 0$, where $a = 1, b = 6$, and $c = 9$.

$$x = \frac{-b \pm \sqrt{b^2 - 4ac}}{2a} = \frac{-6 \pm \sqrt{(6)^2 - 4(1)(9)}}{2(1)} = \frac{-6 \pm \sqrt{36 - 36}}{2} = \frac{-6 \pm \sqrt{0}}{2} = \frac{-6}{2} = -3$$

17. **Method 1: Solve by factoring.**

$(3n - 1)(n + 1) = 0$

$3n - 1 = 0 \qquad or \qquad n + 1 = 0$

$3n - 1 = 0 \qquad\qquad\qquad -1 \quad -1$

$\quad +1 \quad +1 \qquad\qquad\quad n = -1$

$3n = 1$

$\dfrac{3n}{3} = \dfrac{1}{3}$

$n = \dfrac{1}{3}$

Method 2: Solve by the use of the Quadratic Formula.

$3n^2 + 2n - 1 = 0$, where $a = 3, b = 2$, and $c = -1$.

$$n = \frac{-b \pm \sqrt{b^2 - 4ac}}{2a} = \frac{-2 \pm \sqrt{(2)^2 - 4(3)(-1)}}{2(3)} = \frac{-2 \pm \sqrt{4 + 12}}{6} = \frac{-2 \pm \sqrt{16}}{6} = \frac{-2 \pm 4}{6}$$

$$n_1 = \frac{-2 + 4}{6} = \frac{2}{6} = \frac{1}{3} \quad \text{or} \quad n_2 = \frac{-2 - 4}{6} = \frac{-6}{6} = -1$$

19. Before solving the equation for t, rewrite it into the standard quadratic form:

$at^2 + bt + c = 0.$

$5t^2 - t = 1$

$ -1 \quad -1$

$5t^2 - t - 1 = 0$, where $a = 5, b = -1,$ and $c = -1.$

$$t = \frac{-b \pm \sqrt{b^2 - 4ac}}{2a} = \frac{-(-1) \pm \sqrt{(-1)^2 - 4(5)(-1)}}{2(5)} = \frac{1 \pm \sqrt{1+20}}{10} = \frac{1 \pm \sqrt{21}}{10}$$

$$t_1 = \frac{1 + \sqrt{21}}{10} \quad \text{or} \quad t_2 = \frac{1 - \sqrt{21}}{10}$$

21. **Method I: Solve by factoring.**

$x(x - 2) = 0$

$x = 0 \quad or \quad x - 2 = 0$

$ +2 \quad +2$

$ x = 2$

Method 2: Solve by the use of the Quadratic Formula.

$x^2 - 2x = 0$, where $a = 1, b = -2,$ and $c = 0.$

$$x = \frac{-b \pm \sqrt{b^2 - 4ac}}{2a} = \frac{-(-2) \pm \sqrt{(-2)^2 - 4(1)(0)}}{2(1)} = \frac{2 \pm \sqrt{4-0}}{2} = \frac{2 \pm \sqrt{4}}{2} = \frac{2 \pm 2}{2}$$

$$x_1 = \frac{2+2}{2} = \frac{4}{2} = 2 \quad \text{or} \quad x_2 = \frac{2-2}{2} = \frac{0}{2} = 0$$

Section 1.5: The Cartesian Coordinate System

1. (a) $A: (3, 2), \quad B: (9, 6), \quad C: (10, 0), \quad D: (4, -6), \quad E: (8, -4), \quad F: (-6, 5), \quad G: (-2, 1)$

$\quad H: (0, 5), \quad I: (-5, -3), \quad J: (-1, -4), \quad K: (0, -7)$

(b) Points A and B.

3. (a)

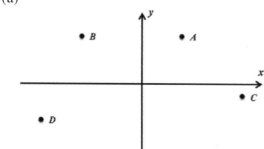

(b)

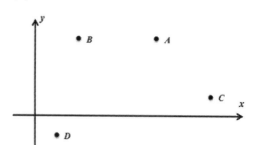

(c)

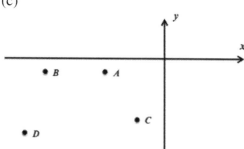

5.

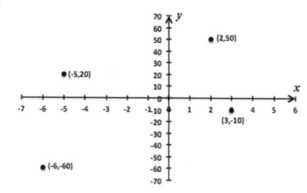

7. (a) The value of the y-coordinate for every point on the x-axis is 0.

(b) The value of the x-coordinate for every point on the y-axis is 0.

9.

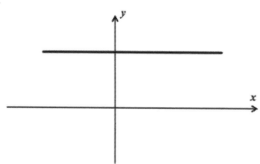

Every point on the line that is parallel to the x-axis has the same y-coordinate value.

Section 1.6: Graphical Solutions to Equations in Two Unknowns

1. If possible, solve the equation for y. We have:

$2x - 3y = 5$

$-2x \qquad - 2x$

$-3y = -2x + 5$

$\dfrac{-3y}{-3} = \dfrac{-2x+5}{-3}$

$y = \dfrac{-2x}{-3} + \dfrac{5}{-3}$

$y = \dfrac{2x}{3} - \dfrac{5}{3}$

To graph the equation, choose arbitrary x-values and then, substitute each x-value into the equation to find its corresponding y-value. Then plot the points on a graph. We have:

For $x = -2$, $y = \dfrac{2(-2)}{3} - \dfrac{5}{3} = \dfrac{-4}{3} - \dfrac{5}{3} = \dfrac{-4-5}{3} = \dfrac{-9}{3} = -3.0$

For $x = -1$, $y = \dfrac{2(-1)}{3} - \dfrac{5}{3} = \dfrac{-2}{3} - \dfrac{5}{3} = \dfrac{-2-5}{3} = \dfrac{-7}{3} = -2.3$

For $x = -0.5$, $y = \dfrac{2(-0.5)}{3} - \dfrac{5}{3} = \dfrac{-1}{3} - \dfrac{5}{3} = \dfrac{-1-5}{3} = \dfrac{-6}{3} = -2.0$

For $x = 0$, $y = \dfrac{2(0)}{3} - \dfrac{5}{3} = 0 - \dfrac{5}{3} = -\dfrac{5}{3} = -1.7$

For $x = 0.5$, $y = \dfrac{2(0.5)}{3} - \dfrac{5}{3} = \dfrac{1}{3} - \dfrac{5}{3} = \dfrac{1-5}{3} = \dfrac{-4}{3} = -1.3$

For $x = 1$, $y = \dfrac{2(1)}{3} - \dfrac{5}{3} = \dfrac{2}{3} - \dfrac{5}{3} = \dfrac{2-5}{3} = \dfrac{-3}{3} = -1$

For $x = 2$, $y = \dfrac{2(2)}{3} - \dfrac{5}{3} = \dfrac{4}{3} - \dfrac{5}{3} = \dfrac{4-5}{3} = \dfrac{-1}{3} = -0.3$

x	y	(x, y)
-2	-3	$(-2, -3)$
-1	-2.3	$(-1, -2.3)$
-0.5	-2	$(-0.5, -2)$
0	-1.7	$(0, -1.7)$
0.5	-1.3	$(0.5, -1.3)$
1	-1	$(1, -1)$
2	-0.3	$(2, -0.3)$

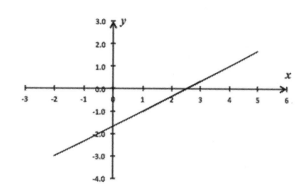

3. If possible, solve the equation for y. We have:

$$6x - 2y = 3$$
$$-6x \qquad -6x$$
$$-2y = -6x + 3$$
$$\frac{-2y}{-2} = \frac{-6x+3}{-2}$$

$$y = \frac{-6x}{-2} + \frac{3}{-2}$$

$$y = 3x - \frac{3}{2}$$

To graph the equation, choose arbitrary x-values and then, substitute each x-value into the equation to find its corresponding y-value. Then plot the points on a graph. We have:

For $x = -2$, $y = 3(-2) - \frac{3}{2} = -6 - 1.5 = -6 + (-1.5) = -7.5$

For $x = -1$, $y = 3(-1) - \frac{3}{2} = -3 - \frac{3}{2} = -3 - 1.5 = -3 + (-1.5) = -4.5$

For $x = -0.5$, $y = 3(-0.5) - \frac{3}{2} = -1.5 - 1.5 = -1.5 + (-1.5) = -3.0$

For $x = 0$, $y = 3(0) - \frac{3}{2} = 0 - 1.5 = -1.5$

For $x = 0.5$, $y = 3(0.5) - \frac{3}{2} = 1.5 - 1.5 = 0$

For $x = 1$, $y = 3(1) - \frac{3}{2} = 3 - 1.5 = 1.5$

For $x = 2$, $y = 3(2) - \frac{3}{2} = 6 - 1.5 = 4.5$

x	y	(x, y)
-2	-7.5	$(-2, -7.5)$
-1	-4.5	$(-1, -4.5)$
-0.5	-3	$(-0.5, -3)$
0	-1.5	$(0, -1.5)$
0.5	0	$(0.5, 0)$
1	1.5	$(1, 1.5)$
2	4.5	$(2, 4.5)$

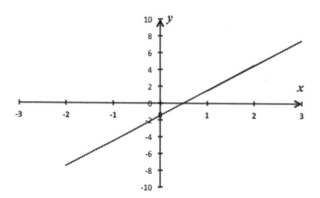

5. To graph the equation, choose arbitrary x-values and then, substitute each x-value into the equation to find its corresponding y-value. Then plot the points on a graph. We have:

For $x = -2$, $y = 2(-2)^2 = 2 \cdot 4 = 8$

For $x = -1$, $y = 2(-1)^2 = 2 \cdot 1 = 2$

For $x = -0.5$, $y = 2(-0.5)^2 = 2 \cdot (.25) = 0.5$

For $x = 0$, $y = 2(0)^2 = 2 \cdot 0 = 0$

For $x = 1$, $y = 2(1)^2 = 2 \cdot 1 = 2$

For $x = 2$, $y = 2(2)^2 = 2 \cdot 4 = 8$

x	y	(x, y)
-2	8	$(-2, 8)$
-1	2	$(-1, 2)$
-0.5	0.5	$(-0.5, 0.5)$
0	0	$(0, 0)$
0.5	0.5	$(0.5, 0.5)$
1	2	$(1, 2)$
2	8	$(2, 8)$

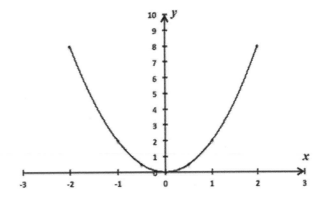

7. To graph the equation, choose arbitrary x-values and then, substitute each x-value into the equation to find its corresponding y-value. Then plot the points on a graph. We have:

For $x = -2$, $y = (-2)^3 - 2(-2)^2 + (-2) = -8 - 8 - 2 = -18$

For $x = -1$, $y = (-1)^3 - 2(-1)^2 + (-1) = -1 - 2 - 1 = -4$

For $x = -0.5$, $y = (-0.5)^3 - 2(-0.5)^2 + (-0.5) = -0.125 - 0.5 - 0.5 = -1.13$

For $x = 0$, $y = (0)^3 - 2(0)^2 + (0) = 0$

For $x = 0.5$, $y = (0.5)^3 - 2(0.5)^2 + 0.5 = 0.125 - 0.5 + 0.5 = 0.13$

For $x = 1$, $y = (1)^3 - 2(1)^2 + 1 = 1 - 2 + 1 = 0$

For $x = 2$, $y = (2)^3 - 2(2)^2 + 2 = 8 - 8 + 2 = 2$

x	$y = x^3 - 2x^2 + x$	(x, y)
-2	-18	$(-2, -18)$
-1	-4	$(-1, -4)$
-0.5	-1.13	$(-0.5, -1.13)$
0	0	$(0, 0)$
0.5	0.13	$(0.5, 0.13)$
1	0	$(1, 0)$
2	2	$(2, 2)$

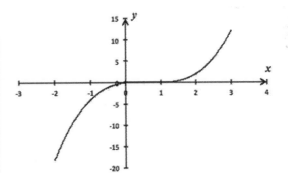

A close-up look at the graph of $y = x^3 - 2x^2 + x$ on the interval [0, 1].

For $x = -1$, $y = (-1)^3 - 2(-1)^2 + (-1) = -1 - 2 - 1 = -4$

For $x = -0.5$, $y = (-0.5)^3 - 2(-0.5)^2 + (-0.5) = -0.125 - 0.5 - 0.5 = -1.13$

For $x = 0$, $y = (0)^3 - 2(0)^2 + (0) = 0$

For $x = 0.25$, $y = (0.25)^3 - 2(0.25)^2 + 0.25 = 0.015625 - 0.125 + 0.25 = 0.14$

For $x = 0.5$, $y = (0.5)^3 - 2(0.5)^2 + 0.5 = 0.125 - 0.5 + 0.5 = 0.13$

For $x = 0.56$, $y = (0.56)^3 - 2(0.56)^2 + 0.56 = 0.175616 - .6272 + 0.56 = 0.11$

For $x = 0.5$, $y = (0.75)^3 - 2(0.75)^2 + 0.75 = 0.421875 - 1.125 + 0.75 = 0.05$

For $x = 1$, $y = (1)^3 - 2(1)^2 + 1 = 1 - 2 + 1 = 0$

For $x = 2$, $y = (2)^3 - 2(2)^2 + 2 = 8 - 8 + 2 = 2$

x	$y = x^3 - 2x^2 + x$	(x, y)
-1	-4	$(-1, -4)$
-0.5	-1.13	$(-1, -1.13)$
0	0	$(0, 0)$
0.25	0.14	$(0.25, 0.14)$
0.5	0.13	$(0.5, 0.13)$
0.56	0.11	$(0.56, 0.11)$
0.75	0.05	$(0.75, 0.05)$
1	0	$(1, 0)$
2	2	$(2, 2)$

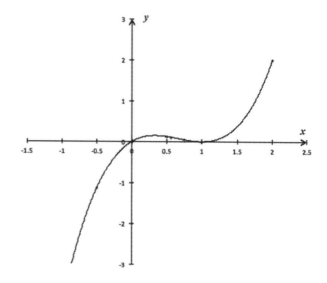

9. If possible, solve the equation for y. We have

$$x^2 + y^2 = 4$$
$$-x^2 \qquad - x^2$$

$$y^2 = 4 - x^2$$

$$y = \pm\sqrt{4 - x^2}$$

To graph the equation, choose arbitrary x-values and then, substitute each x-value into the equation to find its corresponding y-value. Then plot the points on a graph. We have:

For the equation: $y = \sqrt{4 - x^2}$.

For $x = -2$, $y = \sqrt{4 - (-2)^2} = \sqrt{4 - 4} = \sqrt{0} = 0$

For $x = -1.5$, $y = \sqrt{4 - (-1.5)^2} = \sqrt{4 - 2.25} = \sqrt{1.75} = 1.3$

For $x = -1.25$, $y = \sqrt{4 - (-1.25)^2} = \sqrt{4 - 1.6} = \sqrt{2.4} = 1.5$

For $x = -1$, $y = \sqrt{4 - (-1)^2} = \sqrt{4 - 1} = \sqrt{3} = 1.7$

For $x = -0.5$, $y = \sqrt{4 - (-0.5)^2} = \sqrt{4 - 0.25} = \sqrt{3.75} = 1.9$

For $x = 0$, $y = \sqrt{4 - 0^2} = \sqrt{4} = 2$

For $x = 0.5$, $y = \sqrt{4 - (0.5)^2} = \sqrt{4 - 0.25} = \sqrt{3.75} = 1.9$

For $x = 1$, $y = \sqrt{4 - (1)^2} = \sqrt{4 - 1} = \sqrt{3} = 1.7$

For $x = 1.25$, $y = \sqrt{4 - (1.25)^2} = \sqrt{4 - 1.6} = \sqrt{2.4} = 1.5$

For $x = 1.5$, $y = \sqrt{4 - (1.5)^2} = \sqrt{4 - 2.25} = \sqrt{1.75} = 1.3$

For $x = 2$, $y = \sqrt{4 - (2)^2} = \sqrt{4 - 4} = \sqrt{0} = 0$

For the equation: $y = -\sqrt{4 - x^2}$.

For $x = -2$, $y = -\sqrt{4 - (-2)^2} = -\sqrt{4 - 4} = \sqrt{0} = 0$

For $x = -1.5$, $y = -\sqrt{4 - (-1.5)^2} = -\sqrt{4 - 2.25} = -\sqrt{1.75} = -1.3$

For $x = -1.25$, $y = -\sqrt{4 - (-1.25)^2} = -\sqrt{4 - 1.6} = -\sqrt{2.4} = -1.5$

For $x = -1$, $y = -\sqrt{4 - (-1)^2} = -\sqrt{4 - 1} = -\sqrt{3} = -1.7$

For $x = -0.5$, $y = -\sqrt{4 - (-0.5)^2} = -\sqrt{4 - 0.25} = -\sqrt{3.75} = -1.9$

For $x = 0$, $y = -\sqrt{4 - 0^2} = -\sqrt{4} = -2$

For $x = 0.5$, $y = -\sqrt{4 - (0.5)^2} = -\sqrt{4 - 0.25} = -\sqrt{3.75} = -1.9$

For $x = 1$, $y = -\sqrt{4 - (1)^2} = -\sqrt{4 - 1} = -\sqrt{3} = -1.7$

For $x = 1.25$, $y = -\sqrt{4 - (1.25)^2} = -\sqrt{4 - 1.6} = -\sqrt{2.4} = -1.5$

For $x = 1.5$, $y = -\sqrt{4 - (1.5)^2} = -\sqrt{4 - 2.25} = -\sqrt{1.75} = -1.3$

For $x = 2$, $y = -\sqrt{4 - (2)^2} = -\sqrt{4 - 4} = \sqrt{0} = 0$

x	$y = \sqrt{4 - x^2}$	(x, y)
-2	0	$(-2, 0)$
-1.5	1.3	$(-1.5, 1.3)$
-1.25	1.5	$(-1.25, 1.5)$
-1	1.7	$(-1, 1.7)$
-0.5	1.9	$(-0.5, 1.9)$
0	2	$(0, 0)$
0.5	1.9	$(0.5, 1.9)$
1	1.7	$(1, 1.7)$
1.25	1.5	$(1.25, 1.5)$
1.5	1.3	$(1.5, 1.3)$
2	0	$(2, 0)$

x	$y = -\sqrt{4 - x^2}$	(x, y)
-2	0	$(-2, 0)$
-1.5	-1.3	$(-1.5, -1.3)$
-1.25	-1.5	$(-1.25, -1.5)$
-1	-1.7	$(-1, -1.7)$
-0.5	-1.9	$(-0.5, -1.9)$
0	-2	$(0, -2)$
0.5	-1.9	$(0.5, -1.9)$
1	-1.7	$(1, -1.7)$
1.25	-1.5	$(1.25, -1.5)$
1.5	-1.3	$(1.5, -1.3)$
2	0	$(2, 0)$

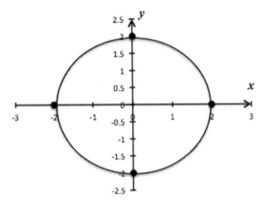

11.

x	$y = x$	(x, y)
-3	-3	$(-3, -3)$
-2	-2	$(-2, -2)$
-1	-1	$(-1, -1)$
-0.5	-0.5	$(-0.5, -0.5)$
0	0	$(0, 0)$
0.5	0.5	$(0.5, 0.5)$
1	1	$(1, 1)$
2	2	$(2, 2)$
3	3	$(3, 3)$

x	$y = -x$	(x, y)
-3	3	$(-3, 3)$
-2	2	$(-2, 2)$
-1	1	$(-1, 1)$
-0.5	0.5	$(-0.5, -0.5)$
0	0	$(0, 0)$
0.5	-0.5	$(0.5, -0.5)$
1	-1	$(1, -1)$
2	-2	$(2, -2)$
3	-3	$(3, -3)$

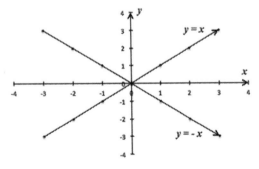

The lines have opposite slopes.

13. The points lie on the graph if they satisfy the equation $y = 3x^2 + 4x + 2$.

For $x = -2$, $y = 3(-2)^2 + 4(-2) + 2 = 3 \cdot 4 - 8 + 2 = 12 - 8 + 2 = 6$.

Therefore, $(-2, 6)$ is on the graph of $y = 3x^2 + 4x + 2$.

For $x = 0$, $y = 3(0)^2 + 4(0) + 2 = 3 \cdot 0 + 0 + 2 = 2$. Therefore, $(0, 2)$ is on the graph of $y = 3x^2 + 4x + 2$.

For $x = 1$, $y = 3(1)^2 + 4(1) + 2 = 3 \cdot 1 + 4 + 2 = 3 + 4 + 2 = 9$. Therefore, $(1, 9)$ is on the graph of $y = 3x^2 + 4x + 2$.

Hence, all three points lie on the graph of $y = 3x^2 + 4x + 2$.

15. **(A) Solve by Graphing**

To graph the equation, choose arbitrary x-values and then, substitute each x-value into the equation to find its corresponding y-value. Then plot the points on a graph. We have:

For the equation $y = 5x^2 - 2$:

For $x = -2$, $y = 5(-2)^2 - 2 = 5 \cdot 4 - 2 = 20 - 2 = 18$

For $x = -1.5$, $y = 5(-1.5)^2 - 2 = 11.25 - 2 = 9.25$

For $x = -1$, $y = 5(-1)^2 - 2 = 5 \cdot 1 - 2 = 5 - 2 = 3$

For $x = -0.5$, $y = 5(-0.5)^2 - 2 = 1.25 - 2 = -0.75$

For $x = 0$, $y = 5(0)^2 - 2 = 5 \cdot 0 - 2 = 0 - 2 = -2$

For $x = 0.5$, $y = 5(0.5)^2 - 2 = 1.25 - 2 = -0.75$

For $x = 1$, $y = 5(1)^2 - 2 = 5 \cdot 1 - 2 = 5 - 2 = 3$

For $x = 1.5$, $y = 5(1.5)^2 - 2 = 11.25 - 2 = 9.25$

For $x = 2$, $y = 5(2)^2 - 2 = 5 \cdot 4 - 2 = 20 - 2 = 18$

For the equation $y = x + 3$:

For $x = -2$, $y = -2 + 3 = 1$

For $x = -1.5$, $y = -1.5 + 3 = 1.5$

For $x = -1$, $y = -1 + 3 = 2$

For $x = -0.5$, $y = -0.5 + 3 = 2.5$

For $x = 0$, $y = 0 + 3 = 3$

For $x = 0.5$, $y = 0.5 + 3 = 3.5$

For $x = 1$, $y = 1 + 3 = 4$

For $x = 1.5$, $y = 1.5 + 3 = 4.5$

For $x = 2$, $y = 2 + 3 = 5$

x	$y = 5x^2 - 2$	(x, y)
-2	18	$(-2, 18)$
-1.5	9.25	$(-1.5, 9.25)$
-1	3	$(-1, 3)$
-0.5	-0.75	$(-0.5, -0.75)$
0	-2	$(0, -2)$
0.5	-0.75	$(0.5, -0.75)$
1	3	$(1, 3)$
1.5	9.25	$(1.5, 9.25)$
2	18	$(2, 18)$

x	$y = x + 3$	(x, y)
-2	1	$(-2, 1)$
-1.5	1.5	$(-1.5, 1.5)$
-1	2	$(-1, 2)$
-0.5	2.5	$(-0.5, 2.5)$
0	3	$(0, 3)$
0.5	3.5	$(0.5, 3.5)$
1	4	$(1, 4)$
1.5	4.5	$(1.5, 4.5)$
2	5	$(2, 5)$

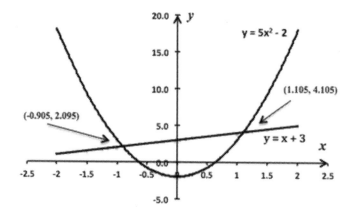

(B) Solve Algebraically

To find the points of intersection, we have to solve the system of equations:

(1) $y = 5x^2 - 2$
(2) $y = x + 3$

Using the Substitution Method, substitute y (as $x + 3$) in equation (1) into equation (2). We have:

$5x^2 - 2 = x + 3$

$-x - 3 \qquad -x - 3$

$5x^2 - 2 - x - 3 = 0$

$5x^2 - x - 5 = 0.$

Use the Quadratic Formula with $a = 5, b = -1$, and $c = -5$ to solve for x. We have:

$$x = \frac{-b \pm \sqrt{b^2 - 4ac}}{2a} = \frac{-(-1) \pm \sqrt{(-1)^2 - 4(5)(-5)}}{2(5)} = \frac{1 \pm \sqrt{1 + 100}}{10} = \frac{1 \pm \sqrt{101}}{10}$$

Therefore, $x_1 = \dfrac{1 + \sqrt{101}}{10} = 1.105$ or $x_2 = \dfrac{1 - \sqrt{101}}{10} = -0.905$

We now need to find the y components for these x-values. We can use either equation (1) or (2) to find y. The results will be the same. Let's choose equation (2) since it is simpler.

For $x = 1.105$, $y = 1.105 + 3 = 4.105$.

For $x = -0.905$, $y = -0.905 + 3 = 2.095$.

Points of intersection: $(1.105, 4.105)$ and $(-0.905, 2.095)$

Section 1.7: Sigma Notation

1. (a) $\displaystyle\sum_{i=1}^{3}(x_i)^2 = x_1^2 + x_2^2 + x_3^2$

(b) $\displaystyle\sum_{i=3}^{11}2x_i = 2x_3 + 2x_4 + 2x_5 + 2x_6 + 2x_7 + 2x_8 + 2x_9 + 2x_{10} + 2x_{11}$

(c) $\displaystyle\sum_{i=1}^{7}(x_i + y_i) = (x_1 + y_1) + (x_2 + y_2) + (x_3 + y_3) + (x_4 + y_4) + (x_5 + y_5) + (x_6 + y_6) + (x_7 + y_7)$

(d) $\displaystyle\sum_{j=99}^{105}(3M_j + 4)$

$= (3M_{99} + 4) + (3M_{100} + 4) + (3M_{101} + 4) + (3M_{102} + 4) + (3M_{103} + 4) + (3M_{104} + 4) + (3M_{105} + 4)$

3. (a) $\displaystyle\sum_{i=2}^{29}(3i)^2$ (c) $\displaystyle\sum_{i=2}^{29}2(3)^i$

(b) $\displaystyle\sum_{i=2}^{29}i(3^2)$ (d) $\displaystyle\sum_{i=2}^{29}(-1)^i 3i^2$

5. (a) $\displaystyle\sum x_i = x_1 + x_2 + x_3 + x_4 + x_5 + x_6 = 0 + 8 + (-2) + 5 + (-3) + 7 = 15$

(b) $\displaystyle\sum y_i = y_1 + y_2 + y_3 + y_4 + y_5 + y_6 = 3 + 2 + 6 + 9 + 10 + 1 = 31$

(c) $\displaystyle\sum(x_i)^2 = (x_1)^2 + (x_2)^2 + (x_3)^2 + (x_4)^2 + (x_5)^2 + (x_6)^2$

$= (0)^2 + (8)^2 + (-2)^2 + (5)^2 + (-3)^2 + (7)^2$

$= 0 + 64 + 4 + 25 + 9 + 49 = 151$

(d) $\sum(x_i-2)=(x_1-2)+(x_2-2)+(x_3-2)+(x_4-2)+(x_5-2)+(x_6-2)$

$=(0-2)+(8-2)+(-2-2)+(5-2)+(-3-2)+(7-2)$

$=-2+6+(-4)+3+(-5)+5=3$

(e) $\sum(x_iy_i)=(x_1y_1)+(x_2y_2)+(x_3y_3)+(x_4y_4)+(x_5y_5)+(x_6y_6)$

$=(0)(3)+(8)(2)+(-2)(6)+(5)(9)+(-3)(10)+(7)(1)$

$=0+16-12+45-30+7=26$

(f) $\left(\sum x_i\right)\left(\sum y_i\right)=(x_1+x_2+x_3+x_4+x_5+x_6)(y_1+y_2+y_3+y_4+y_5+y_6)$

$=(0+8+(-2)+5+(-3)+7)(3+2+6+9+10+1)=(15)(31)=465$

(g) The sums are not equal. Therefore, $\sum(x_iy_i)\neq\left(\sum x_i\right)\left(\sum y_i\right)$

7. (a) $c\left(\sum_{i=1}^{n}x_i\right)=c(x_1+x_2+x_3+\cdots+x_n).$

Using the distributive property, we have:

$=cx_i+cx_2+cx_3+\cdots+cx_n=\sum_{i=1}^{n}(cx_i)$

(b) $\sum_{i=1}^{n}(x_i+y_i)=(x_1+y_1)+(x_2+y_2)+(x_3+y_3)+\cdots+(x_n+y_n).$

Dropping the parenthesis, we have:

$=x_i+y_1+x_2+y_2+x_3+y_3+\cdots+x_n+y_n$

Because addition is commutative, we can rearrange the terms and the sum will still be the same. We have:

$=x_1+x_2+x_3+\cdots+x_n+y_1+y_2+y_3+\cdots+y_n$

$=(x_1+x_2+x_3+\cdots+x_n)+(y_1+y_2+y_3+\cdots+y_n)$

$=\sum_{i=1}^{n}(x_i)+\sum_{i=1}^{n}(y_i)$

(c) $\displaystyle\sum_{i=1}^{m} x_i + \sum_{i=m+1}^{n} x_i = x_1 + x_2 + x_3 + \cdots + x_m + x_{m+1} + x_{m+2} + \cdots + x_n = \sum_{i=1}^{n} x_i$

9. $\displaystyle average = \frac{G_1 + G_2 + G_3 + \cdots + G_n}{n} = \frac{1}{n}\sum_{i=1}^{n} G_i$

Section 1.8: Numerical Considerations

1. $\dfrac{2}{3} = 0.\overline{6} \approx 0.67$

$\dfrac{12}{7} = 1.71428571429 \approx 1.714$

3. $\dfrac{4}{17} = 0.235294117647 \approx 0.24$

$\dfrac{89}{31} = 2.87096774194 \approx 2.871$

5. $\dfrac{89}{31} = 2.87096774194 \approx 2.87$

9. $3.35642\,E3 = 3,356.42$

7. $\dfrac{2}{3} = 0.\overline{6} \approx 0.667$

11. $3.356\,E\text{-}3 = .003356$

$\dfrac{4}{11} = 0.\overline{36} \approx 0.364$

13. $3.3\,E12 = 3,300,000,000,000$

$\dfrac{4}{17} = 0.235294117647 \approx 0.235$

Chapter 2 Equations and Graphs

Section 2.1: Linear Equations

1. If possible, rewrite equations (a) – (j) in the standard form: $Ax + By = C$.

(a) $2x = y$

$\quad -y \quad -y$

$\quad 2x - y = 0$

We see that it is in the form $Ax + By = C$, with $A = 2, B = -1$, and $C = 0$. Therefore, the given equation is linear.

(b) $2x = \dfrac{1}{y}$

$\quad 2x = y^{-1}$

$\quad -y^{-1} \quad -y^{-1}$

$\quad 2x - y^{-1} = 0$

Because the exponent on y is –1 instead of 1, the given equation is not linear.

(c) $xy = 4$

$\quad \dfrac{xy}{y} = \dfrac{4}{y},$ for $y \neq 0$

$\quad x = \dfrac{4}{y}$

$\quad x = 4y^{-1}$

$\quad -4y^{-1} \quad -4y^{-1}$

$\quad x - 4y^{-1} = 0$

Because the exponent on y is –1 instead of 1, the given equation is not linear.

(d) Rewriting $x = 4$ as $x + 0y = 4$, we see that it is in the form $Ax + By = C$, with $A = 1, B = 0$, and $C = 4$. Therefore, the given equation is linear.

(e) $2x - 3y = 0$

We see that it is in the form $Ax + By = C$, with $A = 2, B = -3$, and $C = 0$. Therefore, the given equation is linear.

(f) $y = 4x$

$\quad -4x \quad -4x$

$\quad -4x + y = 0$

We see that it is in the form $Ax + By = C$, with $A = -4, B = 1$, and $C = 0$. Therefore, the given equation is linear.

(g) $y = 4x^2$

$-4x^2 \quad -4x^2$

$-4x^2 + y = 0$

Because the exponent on x is 2 instead of 1, the given equation is not linear.

(h) $x - 2 = 3y$

$-3y \quad\ -3y$

$x - 3y - 2 = 0$

$+2 \quad +2$

$x - 3y = 2$

We see that it is in the form $Ax + By = C$, with $A = 1, B = -3,$ and $C = 2$. Therefore, the given equation is linear.

(i) $\dfrac{1}{x} + \dfrac{1}{y} = 2$

$x^{-1} + y^{-1} = 2$

Because the exponents on x *and* y are –1 instead of 1, the given equation is not linear.

(j) $x = y$

$-y \quad -y$

$x - y = 0$

We see that it is in the form $Ax + By = C$, with $A = 1, B = -1,$ and $C = 0$. Therefore, the given equation is linear.

3. **Part 1:** $V = 6{,}000 - 1{,}500t$

   Part 2: $V = 6{,}000 - 1{,}500t$

$+1{,}500t \quad\ + 1{,}500t$

$V + 1500t = 6{,}000$

We see that it is in the form $Ax + By = C$, with $A = 1, B = 1500,$ and $C = 6{,}000$. Therefore, the given equation is linear.

Section 2.2: Graphing Linear Equations

1. If possible, solve equations (a) – (h) for y. To graph the equation, choose arbitrary x-values and then, substitute each x-value into the equation to find its corresponding y-value. Then, plot these points on a graph. We have:

(a) $2x + 3y = 6$

$\underline{-2x \qquad\quad -2x}$

$3y = -2x + 6$

$\dfrac{3y}{3} = \dfrac{-2x+6}{3}$

$y = \dfrac{-2x}{3} + \dfrac{6}{3}$

$y = -\dfrac{2}{3}x + 2$

For $x = -3$, $y = \dfrac{-2(-3)}{3} + 2 = \dfrac{6}{3} + 2 = 2 + 2 = 4$

For $x = -2$, $y = \dfrac{-2(-2)}{3} + 2 = \dfrac{4}{3} + 2 = \dfrac{4}{3} + \dfrac{6}{3} = \dfrac{10}{3} = 3.33$

For $x = -1$, $y = \dfrac{-2(-1)}{3} + 2 = \dfrac{2}{3} + 2 = \dfrac{2}{3} + \dfrac{6}{3} = \dfrac{8}{3} = 2.67$

For $x = 0$, $y = \dfrac{-2(0)}{3} + 2 = 0 + 2 = 2$

For $x = 1$, $y = \dfrac{-2(1)}{3} + 2 = \dfrac{-2}{3} + 2 = \dfrac{-2}{3} + \dfrac{6}{3} = \dfrac{4}{3} = 1.33$

For $x = 2$, $y = \dfrac{-2(2)}{3} + 2 = \dfrac{-4}{3} + 2 = \dfrac{-4}{3} + \dfrac{6}{3} = \dfrac{2}{3} = 0.67$

For $x = 3$, $y = \dfrac{-2(3)}{3} + 2 = \dfrac{-6}{3} + 2 = -2 + 2 = 0$

x	$y = \dfrac{-2}{3}x+2$	(x, y)
-3	4	$(-3, 4)$
-2	3.33	$(-2, 3.33)$
-1	2.67	$(-1, 2.67)$
0	2	$(0, 2)$
1	1.33	$(1, 1.33)$
2	0.67	$(2, 0.67)$
3	0	$(3, 0)$

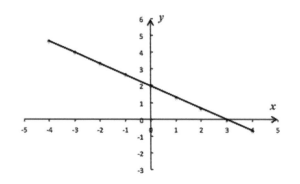

(b) $-2x + 3y = 6$

$\underline{+2x \qquad\quad +2x}$

$3y = 2x + 6$

$\dfrac{3y}{3} = \dfrac{2x+6}{3}$

$y = \dfrac{2x}{3} + \dfrac{6}{3}$

$y = \dfrac{2}{3}x + 2$

For $x = -3$, $y = \dfrac{2(-3)}{3} + 2 = \dfrac{-6}{3} + 2 = -2 + 2 = 0$

For $x = -2$, $y = \dfrac{2(-2)}{3} + 2 = -\dfrac{4}{3} + \dfrac{6}{3} = \dfrac{-4+6}{3} = \dfrac{2}{3} = 0.67$

For $x = -1, y = \frac{2(-1)}{3} + 2 = \frac{-2}{3} + \frac{6}{3} = \frac{-2+6}{3} = \frac{4}{3} = 1.33$

For $x = 0, y = \frac{2(0)}{3} + 2 = 0 + 2 = 2$

For $x = 1, y = \frac{2(1)}{3} + 2 = \frac{2}{3} + 2 = \frac{2}{3} + \frac{6}{3} = \frac{8}{3} = 2.67$

For $x = 2, y = \frac{2(2)}{3} + 2 = \frac{4}{3} + 2 = \frac{4}{3} + \frac{6}{3} = \frac{10}{3} = 3.33$

For $x = 3, y = \frac{2(3)}{3} + 2 = \frac{6}{3} + 2 = 2 + 2 = 4$

x	$y = \frac{2}{3}x+2$	(x,y)
-3	0	$(-3,0)$
-2	0.67	$(-2,0.67)$
-1	1.33	$(-1,1.33)$
0	2	$(0,2)$
1	2.67	$(1,2.67)$
2	3.33	$(2,3.33)$
3	4	$(3,4)$

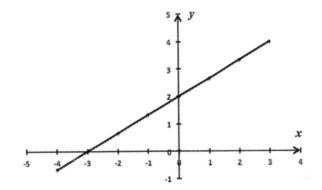

(c) $2x - 3y = 6$

$-2x - 2x$

$-3y = -2x + 6$

$\frac{-3y}{-3} = \frac{-2x+6}{-3}$

$y = \frac{-2x}{-3} + \frac{6}{-3}$

$y = \frac{2}{3}x - 2$

For $x = -3, y = \frac{2(-3)}{3} - 2 = \frac{-6}{3} - 2 = -2 - 2 = -4$

For $x = -2, y = \frac{2(-2)}{3} - 2 = \frac{-4}{3} - 2 = \frac{-4}{3} - \frac{6}{3} = -\frac{10}{3} = -3.33$

For $x = -1, y = \frac{2(-1)}{3} - 2 = \frac{-2}{3} - 2 = \frac{-2}{3} - \frac{6}{3} = -\frac{8}{3} = -2.67$

For $x = 0, y = \frac{2(0)}{3} - 2 = 0 - 2 = -2$

For $x = 1, y = \frac{2(1)}{3} - 2 = \frac{2}{3} - 2 = \frac{2}{3} - \frac{6}{3} = -\frac{4}{3} = -1.33$

For $x = 2, y = \frac{2(2)}{3} - 2 = \frac{4}{3} - 2 = \frac{4}{3} - \frac{6}{3} = -\frac{2}{3} = -0.67$

For $x = 3, y = \frac{2(3)}{3} - 2 = \frac{6}{3} - 2 = \frac{6}{3} - \frac{6}{3} = 0$

x	$y = \frac{2x}{3} - 2$	(x, y)
-3	-4	$(-3, -4)$
-2	-3.33	$(-2, -3.33)$
-1	-2.67	$(-1, -2.67)$
0	0	$(0, -2)$
1	-1.33	$(1, -1.33)$
2	-0.67	$(2, -0.67)$
3	0	$(3, 0)$

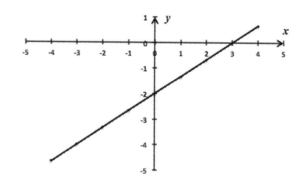

(d) $2x + 3y = -6$

$ -2x -2x$

$3y = -2x - 6$

$\frac{3y}{3} = \frac{-2x - 6}{3}$

$y = \frac{-2x}{3} - \frac{6}{3}$

$y = -\frac{2}{3}x - 2$

For $x = -3$, $y = \frac{-2(-3)}{3} - 2 = \frac{6}{3} - 2 = 2 - 2 = 0$

For $x = -2$, $y = \frac{-2(-2)}{3} - 2 = \frac{4}{3} - 2 = \frac{4}{3} - \frac{6}{3} = -\frac{2}{3} = -0.67$

For $x = -1$, $y = \frac{-2(-1)}{3} - 2 = \frac{2}{3} - 2 = \frac{2}{3} - \frac{6}{3} = -\frac{4}{3} = -1.33$

For $x = 0$, $y = \frac{-2(0)}{3} - 2 = 0 - 2 = -2$

For $x = 1$, $y = \frac{-2(1)}{3} - 2 = \frac{-2}{3} - 2 = \frac{-2}{3} - \frac{6}{3} = -\frac{8}{3} = -2.67$

For $x = 2$, $y = \frac{-2(2)}{3} - 2 = \frac{-4}{3} - 2 = \frac{-4}{3} - \frac{6}{3} = -\frac{10}{3} = -3.33$

For $x = 3$, $y = \frac{-2(3)}{3} - 2 = \frac{-6}{3} - 2 = -2 - 2 = -4$

x	$y = -\frac{2}{3}x - 2$	(x, y)
-3	0	$(-3, 0)$
-2	-0.67	$(-2, -0.67)$
-1	-1.33	$(-1, -1.33)$
0	-2	$(0, -2)$
1	-2.67	$(1, -2.67)$
2	-3.33	$(2, -3.33)$
3	-4	$(3, -4)$

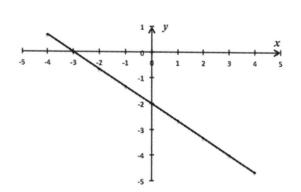

(e) $3x + 2y = 6$

$\underline{-3x \qquad -3x}$

$2y = -3x + 6$

$\dfrac{2y}{2} = \dfrac{-3x+6}{2}$

$y = \dfrac{-3x}{2} + \dfrac{6}{2}$

$y = -\dfrac{3}{2}x + 3$

For $x = -3, y = \dfrac{-3(-3)}{2} + 3 = \dfrac{9}{2} + 3 = \dfrac{9}{2} + \dfrac{6}{2} = \dfrac{15}{2} = 7.5$

For $x = -2, y = \dfrac{-3(-2)}{2} + 3 = \dfrac{6}{2} + 3 = 3 + 3 = 6$

For $x = -1, y = \dfrac{-3(-1)}{2} + 3 = \dfrac{3}{2} + 3 = \dfrac{3}{2} + \dfrac{6}{2} = \dfrac{9}{2} = 4.5$

For $x = 0, y = \dfrac{-30}{2} + 3 = 0 + 3 = 3$

For $x = 1, y = \dfrac{-3(1)}{2} + 3 = \dfrac{-3}{2} + \dfrac{6}{2} = \dfrac{3}{2} = 1.5$

For $x = 2, y = \dfrac{-3(2)}{2} + 3 = \dfrac{-6}{2} + 3 = -3 + 3 = 0$

For $x = 3, y = \dfrac{-3(3)}{2} + 3 = \dfrac{-9}{2} + \dfrac{6}{2} = \dfrac{-9+6}{2} = \dfrac{-3}{2} - 1.5$

x	$y = -\dfrac{3}{2}x+3$	(x,y)
-3	7.5	$(-3, 7.5)$
-2	6	$(-2, 6)$
-1	4.5	$(-1, 4.5)$
0	3	$(0, 3)$
1	1.5	$(1, 1.5)$
2	0	$(2, 0)$
3	-1.5	$(3, -1.5)$

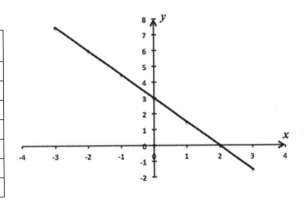

(f) $x = 7$ is a vertical line through the point $(7, 0)$.

x	y	(x,y)
7	-2	$(7, -2)$
7	-1	$(7, -1)$
7	0	$(7, 0)$
7	1	$(7, 1)$
7	2	$(7, 2)$
7	3	$(7, 3)$
7	4	$(7, 4)$

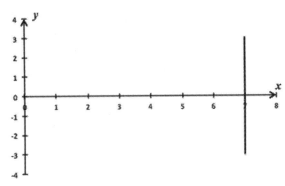

(g) $10x - 5y = 50$

$-10x -10x$

$-5y = -10x + 50$

$\dfrac{-5y}{-5} = \dfrac{-10x+50}{-5}$

$y = \dfrac{-10x}{-5} + \dfrac{50}{-5}$

$y = 2x - 10$

For $x = -3, y = 2(-3) - 10 = -6 - 10 = -16$

For $x = -2, y = 2(-2) - 10 = -4 - 10 = -14$

For $x = -1, y = 2(-1) - 10 = -2 - 10 = -12$

For $x = 0, y = 2(0) - 10 = 0 - 10 = -10$

For $x = 1, y = 2(1) - 10 = 2 - 10 = -8$

For $x = 2, y = 2(2) - 10 = 4 - 10 = -6$

For $x = 3, y = 2(3) - 10 = 6 - 10 = -4$

x	$y = 2x - 10$	(x, y)
-3	-16	$(-3, -6)$
-2	-14	$(-2, -14)$
-1	-12	$(-1, -12)$
0	-10	$(0, -10)$
1	-8	$(1, -8)$
2	-6	$(2, -6)$
3	-4	$(3, -4)$

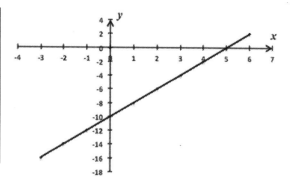

(h) $x = y$ or $y = x$

x	$y = x$	(x, y)
-3	-3	$(-3, -3)$
-2	-2	$(-2, -2)$
-1	-1	$(-1, -1)$
0	0	$(0, 0)$
1	1	$(1, 1)$
2	2	$(2, 2)$
3	3	$(3, 3)$

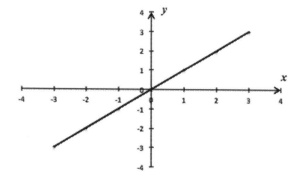

3. Given $S = 10$, we are to determine E. Substituting $S = 10$ into the given equation and solve for E. We have:

$$10 = 2E + 2.14$$
$$-2.14 \qquad - 2.14$$
$$7.86 = 2E$$

$$\frac{7.86}{2} = \frac{2E}{2}$$
$$E = \$3.93 \ million$$

5. The price, p, at which the number of cans ceased to be saleable is when $A = 0$. That is,

$$0 = 200 - p$$
$$+p \qquad + p$$
$$p = 200 \ cents$$

Section 2.3: Properties of Straight Lines

1. If possible, rewrite equations (a) – (h) in the form: $y = mx + b$.

(a) $2x + 3y = 6$

$\quad -2x \qquad - 2x$

$\quad 3y = -2x + 6$

$\quad \dfrac{3y}{3} = \dfrac{-2x+6}{3}$

$y = \dfrac{-2x}{3} + \dfrac{6}{3}$

$y = -\dfrac{2}{3}x + 2.$

Therefore, the slope $m = -\dfrac{2}{3}$

(b) $-2x + 3y = 6$

$\quad +2x \qquad + 2x$

$\quad 3y = 2x + 6$

$\quad \dfrac{3y}{3} = \dfrac{2x+6}{3}$

$y = \dfrac{2x}{3} + \dfrac{6}{3}$

$y = \dfrac{2}{3}x + 2.$

Therefore, the slope $m = \dfrac{2}{3}$

(c) $2x - 3y = 6$

$\quad -2x \qquad - 2x$

$\quad -3y = -2x + 6$

$\quad \dfrac{-3y}{-3} = \dfrac{-2x+6}{-3}$

$y = \dfrac{-2x}{-3} + \dfrac{6}{-3}$

$y = \dfrac{2}{3}x - 2$

Therefore, the slope $m = \dfrac{2}{3}$.

(d) $2x + 3y = -6$

$\quad -2x \qquad - 2x$

$\quad 3y = -2x - 6$

$\quad \dfrac{3y}{3} = \dfrac{-2x-6}{3}$

$y = \dfrac{-2x}{3} - \dfrac{6}{3}$

$y = -\dfrac{2}{3}x - 2$

Therefore, the slope $m = -\dfrac{2}{3}$

(e) $3x + 2y = 6$

$-3x - 3x$

$2y = -3x + 6$

$\dfrac{2y}{2} = \dfrac{-3x+6}{2}$

$y = \dfrac{-3x}{2} + \dfrac{6}{2}$

$y = -\dfrac{3}{2}x + 3$

Therefore, the slope $m = -\dfrac{3}{2}$.

(f) $x = 7$ is a vertical line through the point $(7, 0)$. Therefore, it's slope is undefined or ∞.

(g) $10x - 5y = 50$

$-10x - 10x$

$-5y = -10x + 50$

$\dfrac{-5y}{-5} = \dfrac{-10x+50}{-5}$

$y = \dfrac{-10x}{-5} + \dfrac{50}{-5}$

$y = 2x - 10$

Therefore, the slope $m = 2$.

(h) $x = y$ or $y = x + 0$

Therefore, the slope $m = 1$.

3. Let $t = 0$ stands for January, $t = 1$ for February, and so on. Then the y-intercept of the line is $(0, 1)$ and another point on the line is $(11, 3)$. Using $m = \dfrac{y_2 - y_1}{x_2 - x_1}$ with $(x_1, y_1) = (0, 1)$ and $(x_2, y_2) = (11, 3)$, we have:

$$m = \dfrac{y_2 - y_1}{x_2 - x_1} = \dfrac{3 - 1}{11 - 0} = \dfrac{2}{11}$$

Therefore, the equation relating attendance, A, to time t (in months) is $A = \dfrac{2}{11}t + 1$.

5. **Part 1:**

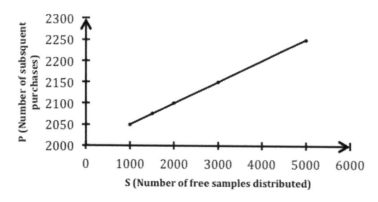

Part 2: Obviously the graph indicates a straight-line relationship between P and S. So, we seek an equation of the form $P = mS + b$. Using $m = \dfrac{y_2 - y_1}{x_2 - x_1}$ with $(x_1, y_1) = (1000, 2050)$ and $(x_2, y_2) = (2000, 2100)$, we have:

$$m = \frac{y_2 - y_1}{x_2 - x_1} = \frac{2100 - 2050}{2000 - 1000} = \frac{50}{1000} = \frac{1}{20} = 0.05$$

To obtain b, we substitute any one of the data points, say $S = 1,000$ and $P = 2,050$ into $P = 0.05S + b$ to find b. We have:

$2,050 = 0.05(1,000) + b$

$2,050 = 50 + b$

$\quad -50 \quad -50$

$\quad\quad b = 2,000$

Therefore, $P = \frac{1}{20}S + 2,000$ or $P = 0.05S + 2,000$

Section 2.4: Break-Even Analysis

1. (a) $C = ax + F$
   $\quad C = 10x + 20,000$

   (b) $R = px$
   $\quad R = 12x$

   (c) $P = R - C$

   $\quad P = 12x - (10x + 20,000) = 12x - 10x - 20,000 = 2x - 20,000$

   For $x = 3,000$, $P = 2(3,000) - 20,000 = 6,000 - 20,000 = -\$14,000$.

   (d) $BEP = x = \dfrac{F}{p-a} = \dfrac{\$20,000}{\$12 - \$10} = \dfrac{\$20,000}{\$2} = 10,000$ textbooks

3. (a) $BEP = x = \dfrac{F}{p-a} = \dfrac{\$15,000}{\$12 - \$2} = \dfrac{\$15,000}{\$10} = 1,500$ staplers

   (b) To graph the equations $R = 12x$ and $C = 2x + 15,000$, choose arbitrary x-values and then, substitute each x-value into the equation to find its corresponding y-value. Then plot the points on a graph. We have:

   For the equation: $y = R = 12x$

   For $x = 0$, $y = 12(0) = 0$

   For $x = 500$, $y = 12(500) = 6,000$

   For $x = 1,000$, $y = 12(1,000) = 12,000$

   For $x = 1,500$, $y = 12(1,500) = 18,000$

   For $x = 2,000$, $y = 12(2,000) = 24,000$

For the equation: $y = C = 2x + 15,000$

For $x = 0$,　　$y = 2(0) + 15000 = 15,000$

For $x = 500$,　$y = 2(500) + 15000 = 1,000 + 15,000 = 16,000$

For $x = 1,000$, $y = 2(1,000) + 15000 = 2,000 + 15,000 = 17,000$

For $x = 1,500$, $y = 2(1,500) + 15000 = 3,000 + 15,000 = 18,000$

For $x = 2,000$, $y = 2(2,000) + 15000 = 4,000 + 15,000 = 19,000$

x	$R = 12x$	(x, y)
0	0	(0, 0)
500	6000	(500, 6000)
1000	12000	(1000, 12000
1500	18000	(1500, 18000)
2000	20000	(2000, 24000)

x	$C = 2x + 15000$	(x, y)
0	15000	(0, 15000)
500	16000	(500, 16000)
1000	17000	(1000, 17000)
1500	18000	(1500, 18000)
2000	19000	(2000, 19000)

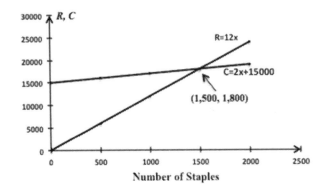

The break-even point is where the lines intersect: (1,500, 18,000).

5. (a) BEP $= x = \dfrac{F}{p-a} = \dfrac{\$15,000}{\$1.75-\$0.15} = \dfrac{\$15,000}{\$1.60} = 9{,}375$ bulbs

(b) BEP $= x = \dfrac{F}{p-a} = \dfrac{\$15,000}{\$2.50-\$0.15} = \dfrac{\$15,000}{\$2.35} = 6{,}383$ bulbs

(c) Yes, because revenue increases faster if the selling price is lower.

7. We are to determine the variable cost, a, given BEP (or x) = 120, selling cost $p = 25$, and fixed cost $F = \$1,920$.

$$\text{BEP} = x = \dfrac{F}{p-a}$$

$$120 = \dfrac{1{,}920}{25-a}$$

$$120(25 - a) = \frac{1,920}{25-a}(25 - a)$$

$$120(25 - a) = \frac{1,920}{\cancel{25-a}}\cancel{(25 - a)}$$

$$120(25 - a) = 1,920$$

$$3,000 - 120a = 1,920$$

$$\begin{array}{ll} -3,000 & -3,000 \end{array}$$

$$-120a = -1,080$$

$$\frac{-120a}{-120} = \frac{-1,080}{-120}$$

$$a = 9$$

The variable cost per bookend is \$9.00.

Section 2.5: Quadratic Equations

1. If possible, rewrite equations (a) – (h) into the form $y = ax^2 + bx + c$.

(a) $x^2 - x = y$

$y = x^2 - x$

The given equation is a quadratic equation with x as the quadratic variable with $a = 1, b = -2$, and $c = 0$.

(b) $y^4 = 3$

$(y^4)^{1/4} = \pm 3^{1/4}$

$y = \pm \sqrt[4]{3}$

The given equation is not a quadratic equation.

(c) This equation is a quadratic equation with , $a = 1, b = -2, and\ c = 2$.

(d) Solve the equation for y. We have:

$y - x^2 = 0$

$+ x^2 \quad + x^2$

$y = x^2$

The given equation is a quadratic equation with x as the quadratic variable with $a = 1, b = 0$, and $c = 0$.

(e) Solve the equation for y. We have: $y = -x + 3$. The given equation is not a quadratic equation since the exponent on x is not 2.

(f) Solve the given equation for d. We have:

$$2d + 5 = n^2$$
$$\quad -5 \quad\; -5$$
$$2d = n^2 - 5$$

$$\frac{2d}{2} = \frac{n^2-5}{2}$$

$$d = \frac{n^2}{2} - \frac{5}{2}$$

The given equation is a quadratic equation with n as the quadratic variable with $a = \frac{1}{2}, b = 0$, and $c = -\frac{5}{2}$.

(g) The given equation is a quadratic equation with S as the quadratic variable with $a = 2, b = 0$, and $c = 0$.

(h) Solve the given equation for y. We have:

$$\left(y^{1/2}\right)^2 = x^2, \qquad x \geq 0 \text{ and } y \geq 0$$
$$y = x^2, \qquad\qquad x \geq 0 \text{ and } y \geq 0$$

The given equation is a quadratic equation with x as the quadratic variable with $a = 1, b = 0$, and $c = 0$.

3. For (a) – (f), the solution(s) to $ax^2 + bx + c = 0$ is (are): $x = \dfrac{-b \pm \sqrt{b^2 - 4ac}}{2a}$.

(a) **Method 1: Solve by Factoring**

$$(x - 3)(x + 2) = 0$$
$$x - 3 = 0 \quad or \quad x + 2 = 0$$
$$+3 \quad +3 \qquad\quad -2 \quad -2$$
$$x = 3 \quad or \ x = -2$$

Method 2: Use the Quadratic Formula

Here, $a = 1, b = -1$, and $c = -6$.

$$x = \frac{-b \pm \sqrt{b^2 - 4ac}}{2a} = \frac{-(-1) \pm \sqrt{(-1)^2 - 4(1)(-6)}}{2(1)} = \frac{1 \pm \sqrt{1+24}}{2} = \frac{1 \pm \sqrt{25}}{2} = \frac{1 \pm 5}{2}$$

$$x_1 = \frac{1+5}{2} = \frac{6}{2} = 3 \ \text{ or } \ x_2 = \frac{1-5}{2} = \frac{-4}{2} = -2$$

(b) Here, $a = 3$, $b = -2$, and $c = -5$.

$$x = \frac{-b \pm \sqrt{b^2 - 4ac}}{2a} = \frac{-(-2) \pm \sqrt{(-2)^2 - 4(3)(-5)}}{2(3)} = \frac{2 \pm \sqrt{4 + 60}}{6} = \frac{2 \pm \sqrt{64}}{6} = \frac{2 \pm 8}{6}$$

$$x_1 = \frac{2+8}{6} = \frac{10}{6} = \frac{5}{3} \quad \text{or} \quad x_2 = \frac{2-8}{6} = \frac{-6}{6} = -1$$

(c) Here, $a = 4$, $b = 0$, and $c = -7$.

$$x = \frac{-0 \pm \sqrt{(0)^2 - 4(4)(-7)}}{2(4)} = \frac{0 \pm \sqrt{0 + 112}}{8} = \frac{\pm\sqrt{112}}{8} = \frac{\pm\sqrt{16 \cdot 7}}{8} = \frac{\pm 4\sqrt{7}}{8} = \frac{\pm\sqrt{7}}{2}$$

$$x_1 = \frac{\sqrt{7}}{2} \quad \text{or} \quad x_2 = -\frac{\sqrt{7}}{2}$$

(d) Since the equation is not factorable, we will use the quadratic formula to solve for x. Since $a = \frac{1}{3}$, it will be difficult to work with. Therefore, we will remove the fraction in the equation by multiplying both sides by 3. We have:

$$3\left(\frac{1}{3}x^2 - x - 1\right) = 3 \cdot 0$$

$$3 \cdot \frac{1}{3}x^2 - 3x - 3 = 0$$

$$x^2 - 3x - 3 = 0$$

Here, $a = 1$, $b = -3$, and $c = -3$.

$$x = \frac{-b \pm \sqrt{b^2 - 4ac}}{2a} = \frac{(-3) \pm \sqrt{(-3)^2 - 4(1)(-3)}}{2(1)} = \frac{3 \pm \sqrt{9 + 12}}{2} = \frac{3 \pm \sqrt{21}}{2}$$

$$x_1 = \frac{3 + \sqrt{21}}{2} \quad \text{or} \quad x_2 = \frac{3 - \sqrt{21}}{2}$$

(e) First, rewrite $x^2 - x = 4$ in the standard form: $ax^2 + bx + c = 0$. We have:

$$x^2 - x = 4$$
$$ -4 \quad -4$$
$$x^2 - x - 4 = 0$$

Since the quadratic equation is not factorable, we will use the quadratic formula to solve for x. Here, $a = 1$, $b = -1$, and $c = -4$.

$$x = \frac{-b \pm \sqrt{b^2 - 4ac}}{2a} = \frac{-(-1) \pm \sqrt{(-1)^2 - 4(1)(-4)}}{2(1)} = \frac{1 \pm \sqrt{1 + 16}}{2} = \frac{1 \pm \sqrt{17}}{2}$$

$$x_1 = \frac{1+\sqrt{17}}{2} \quad \text{or} \quad x_2 = \frac{1-\sqrt{17}}{2}$$

(f) Since the quadratic equation is not factorable, we will use the quadratic formula to solve for x. Here, $a = 3$, $b = -12$, and $c = 6$.

$$x = \frac{-b \pm \sqrt{b^2 - 4ac}}{2a} = \frac{-(-12) \pm \sqrt{(-12)^2 - 4(3)(6)}}{2(3)} = \frac{12 \pm \sqrt{144 - 72}}{6}$$

$$= \frac{12 \pm \sqrt{72}}{6} = \frac{12 \pm \sqrt{36 \cdot 2}}{6} = \frac{12 \pm 6\sqrt{2}}{6} = \frac{6(2 \pm \sqrt{2})}{6} = 2 \pm \sqrt{2}$$

$$x_1 = 2 + \sqrt{2} \quad \text{or} \quad x_2 = 2 - \sqrt{2}$$

5. (a) $t = 3$ and $P = 25{,}000$

$$V = (-0.005 \cdot 3^2 - 0.05 \cdot 3 + 0.8)(25{,}000) = (-0.045 - 0.15 + 0.8)(25{,}000)$$
$$= 0.605(25{,}000) = \$15{,}125$$

(b) $t = 0$ and $P = 25{,}000$

$$V = \left(-0.005 \cdot 0^2 - 0.05 \cdot 0 + 0.8\right)(25{,}000) = (0 - 0 + 0.8)(25{,}000) = 0.8(25{,}000)$$
$$= \$20{,}000$$

(c) $V = 12{,}800$ and $P = 40{,}000$

$$12{,}800 = (-0.005t^2 - 0.05t + 0.8)(40{,}000)$$
$$(-0.005t^2 - 0.05t + .8)(40{,}000) = 12{,}800$$
$$-200t^2 - 2000t + 32{,}000 = 12{,}800$$
$$\qquad\qquad\quad -12{,}800 \quad\ -12{,}800$$
$$-200t^2 - 2{,}000t + 19{,}200 = 0$$
$$-200(t^2 + 10t - 96) = 0$$
$$\frac{-200(t^2 + 10t - 96)}{-200} = \frac{0}{-200}$$
$$t^2 + 10t - 96 = 0$$

Method 1: Solve by Factoring

$$(t + 16)(t - 6) = 0$$

$$
\begin{array}{lcl}
t + 16 = 0 & \quad or \quad & t - 6 = 0 \\
\quad -16 \quad -16 & & \quad +6 \quad +6 \\
t = -16 & & t = 6
\end{array}
$$

Since time is positive, the only solution is $t = 6$ years.

Method 2: Use the Quadratic Formula

Here, $a = 1, b = 10, and\ c = -96.$ We have:

$$t = \frac{-(10) \pm \sqrt{(10)^2 - 4(1)(-96)}}{2(1)} = \frac{-10 \pm \sqrt{100 + 384}}{2}$$

$$= \frac{-10 \pm \sqrt{484}}{2} = \frac{-10 \pm 22}{2}$$

$$t_1 = \frac{-10 + 22}{2} = \frac{12}{2} = 6 \quad \text{or} \quad t_2 = \frac{-10 - 22}{2} = \frac{-32}{2} = -16$$

Since time is positive, the only solution is $t = 6$ years.

Section 2.6: Polynomial Equations

1. (a) $y = x^5 - 2x^2$ represents a fifth-degree polynomial curve having the form

$y = a_5 x^5 + a_4 x^4 + a_3 x^3 + a_2 x^2 + a_1 x + a_0$, where $a_5 = 1, a_4 = 0, a_3 = 0,$
$a_2 = -2, a_1 = 0, and\ a_0 = 0.$

(b) Solving the equation for y, we have:

$$(y^2)^{1/2} = \pm(x^3 + 1)^{1/2}$$

$$y = \pm\sqrt{x^3 + 1}$$

Therefore, the given equation does not represent a polynomial curve.

(c) Solving the equation for y, we have:

$$y - x^2 = x^4$$
$$+ x^2 \quad + x^2$$
$$y = x^4 + x^2$$

Therefore, $y = x^4 + x^2$ represents a fourth-degree polynomial curve having the form

$y = a_4 x^4 + a_3 x^3 + a_2 x^2 + a_1 x + a_0$, where $a_4 = 1, a_3 = 0, a_2 = 1, a_1 = 0$ and $a_0 = 0.$

(d) Solving the equation for y, we have:

$$(y^5)^{1/5} = 1^{1/5}$$

$y = 1 = x^0.$ This is a constant polynomial of degree 0.

(e) $y = x^2 - 2x + 5$ represents a second-degree polynomial curve having the form

$y = a_2 x^2 + a_1 x + a_0$, where $a_2 = 1, a_1 = -2,$ and $a_0 = 5.$

(f) $y = \sqrt{x} + 1 = x^{1/2} + 1$ does not represent a polynomial curve, because the exponent on x is $\frac{1}{2}$, which is not a nonnegative integer.

Section 2.7: Exponential Equations

1. $y = 2(7^x)$ is an exponential equation with $a = 2$ and $b = 7$.

3. $y = 2(x^7)$ is not an exponential equation because the base is x and not a fixed nonnegative number.

5. Using the Power Rule for exponents, we can rewrite the equation $y = (7^x)^2$ to $y = 7^{2x}$. Applying the Product Rule to $y = 7^{2x}$, we can rewrite it to $y = (7^2)^x = 49^x$. Therefore, $y = 7^{2x}$ is an exponential equation with $a = 1$ and $b = 49$.

7. $y = 2\left(-\frac{1}{2}\right)^x$ is not an exponential equation because the base $b = -\frac{1}{2}$ is negative.

9. $y = 9(1.1)^x$ is an exponential equation with $a = 9$ and $b = 1.1$.

11. (a) $Number\ of\ Bacteria = 100e^{0.2(10)} = 100(7.3891) = 902.5 = 739$ bacteria.

(b) $Number\ of\ Bacteria = 100e^{0.2(24)} = 100(121.5104) = 12{,}151$ bacteria.

(c) $Number\ of\ Bacteria = 100e^{0.2(36)} = 100(1{,}339.4308) = 133{,}943$ bacteria.

(d) $Number\ of\ Bacteria = 100e^{0.2(48)} = 100(14{,}764.7816) = 1{,}476{,}478$ bacteria.

13. (a) $Remaining\ Material = 100e^{-0.00012(1{,}000)} = 100(0.8869) = 88.69$ grams.

(b) $Remaining\ Material = 250e^{-0.00012(500)} = 250(0.9418) = 235.45$ grams.

Chapter 3: The Mathematics of Finance

Section 3.1: Compound Interest

1. (a) $i = \frac{r}{1} = \frac{0.02}{1} = 0.02$, $n = 1(4) = 4, P(0) = \$2,000$

  (b) $P(n) = (1+i)^n P(0) = P(0)(1+i)^n$

   $P(4) = P(4) = \$2,000(1+.02)^4 = \$2,000(1.02)^4 = \$2,164.86$

3. $i = \frac{r}{1} = \frac{0.04}{1} = 0.04$, $n = 1(3) = 3, P(0) = \$2,500$

  $P(n) = (1+i)^n P(0) = P(0)(1+i)^n$

  $P(3) = P(3) = \$2,500(1+.04)^3 = \$2,500(1.04)^3 = \$2,812.16$

5. $i = \frac{r}{4} = \frac{0.05}{4} = 0.0125, n = 4(3) = 12, P(0) = \$2,500$

  $P(n) = (1+i)^n P(0) = P(0)(1+i)^n$

  $P(12) = \$2,500(1+0.0125)^{12} = \$2,500(1.0125)^{12} = \$2,901.89$

7. $i = \frac{r}{1} = \frac{0.025}{1} = 0.025, n = 1(25) = 25, P(0) = \$1,000$

  $P(n) = (1+i)^n P(0) = P(0)(1+i)^n$

  $P(25) = \$1,000(1+.025)^{25} = \$1,000(1.025)^{25} = \$1,853.94$

9. $i = \frac{r}{12} = \frac{0.015}{12} = 0.00125, n = 3(12) = 36, P(0) = \$2,900$

  $P(n) = (1+i)^n P(0) = P(0)(1+i)^n$

  $P(36) = \$2,900(1+.00125)^{36} = \$2,900(1.00125)^{36} = \$3,033.40$

11. $i = \frac{r}{365} = \frac{0.025}{365}, n = 365(4) = 1,460, P(0) = \$3,500$

  $P(n) = (1+i)^n P(0) = P(0)(1+i)^n$

  $P(1,460) = \$3,500\left(1+\frac{.025}{365}\right)^{1,460} = \$3,868.08$

13. $i = \frac{r}{365} = \frac{0.03}{365}, n = 365(3) = 1,095, P(0) = \$2,500$

  $P(n) = (1+i)^n P(0) = P(0)(1+i)^n$

  $P(1,095) = \$2,500\left(1+\frac{.03}{356}\right)^{1,095} = \$2,735.43$

Section 3.2: Comparing Investment Alternatives

1. (a) $FV = P(0)(1 + i)^n = P(0)\left(1 + \frac{r}{1}\right)^n = \$5{,}000\left(1 + \frac{0.04}{1}\right)^{1\cdot 10}$

$= \$5{,}000(1.04)^{10} = \$7{,}401.22$

(b) $FV = P(0)(1 + i)^n = P(0)\left(1 + \frac{r}{2}\right)^n = \$5{,}000\left(1 + \frac{0.04}{2}\right)^{2\cdot 10}$

$= \$5{,}000(1.02)^{20} = \$7{,}429.74$

(c) $FV = P(0)(1 + i)^n = P(0)\left(1 + \frac{r}{4}\right)^n = \$5{,}000\left(1 + \frac{0.04}{4}\right)^{4\cdot 10}$

$= \$5{,}000(1.01)^{40} = \$7{,}444.32$

(d) $FV = P(0)(1 + i)^n = P(0)\left(1 + \frac{r}{365}\right)^n = \$5{,}000\left(1 + \frac{0.04}{365}\right)^{365\cdot 10}$

$= \$5{,}000\left(1 + \frac{0.04}{365}\right)^{3650} = \$7{,}458.96$

3. $FV = P(0)(1 + i)^n = P(0)\left(1 + \frac{r}{4}\right)^n = \$12{,}000\left(1 + \frac{0.05}{4}\right)^{4\cdot 7}$

$= \$12{,}000(1 + .0125)^{28} = \$12{,}000(1.0125)^{28} = \$16{,}991.91$

5. **At 2%:** $FV = P(0)(1 + i)^n = P(0)\left(1 + \frac{r}{4}\right)^n = \$1{,}000\left(1 + \frac{0.02}{4}\right)^{4\cdot 1}$

$= \$1{,}000(1.005)^4 = \$1{,}020.15$

At 4%: $FV = P(0)(1 + i)^n = P(0)\left(1 + \frac{r}{1}\right)^n = \$1{,}000\left(1 + \frac{.04}{1}\right)^{1}$

$= \$1{,}000(1.04) = \$1{,}040$

Therefore, *assuming equal credit risk for both alternative*, the 4% annually is the better investment alternative.

7. (a) $PV = (1 + i)^{-n}FV = FV(1 + i)^{-n} = FV\left(1 + \frac{r}{1}\right)^{-n} = \$15{,}000\left(1 + \frac{0.02}{1}\right)^{-8\cdot 1}$

$= \$12{,}802.36$

(b) $PV = FV(1 + i)^{-n} = FV\left(1 + \frac{r}{1}\right)^{-n} = \$15{,}000\left(1 + \frac{0.04}{1}\right)^{-8\cdot 1}$

$= \$15{,}000(1 + .04)^{-8} = \$10{,}960.35$

(c) $V = FV(1 + i)^{-n} = FV\left(1 + \frac{r}{1}\right)^{-n} = \$15{,}000\left(1 + \frac{.08}{1}\right)^{-8\cdot 1}$

$= \$15{,}000(1.08)^{-8} = \$8{,}104.03$

(d) The Present Value of a Future Value amount goes down (that is, decreases) as the interest rate increases.

9. $PV = FV(1 + i)^{-n} = FV\left(1 + \frac{r}{2}\right)^{-n} = \$10,000\left(1 + \frac{0.04}{2}\right)^{-4.5(2)} = \$10,000(1.02)^{-9}$

$\quad = \$8,367.55$

11. Calculate the future value of \$10,000 invested at 4% for 3 years compounding quarterly.

$\quad FV = P(0)(1 + i)^n = P(0)\left(1 + \frac{r}{4}\right)^n = \$10,000\left(1 + \frac{0.04}{4}\right)^{4\cdot3} = \$10,000(1.01)^{12}$

$\quad = \$11,268.25.$

In a friend's business she will receive \$12,000 in three years. Investing at 4% account yield \$11,268.25. Therefore, ***assuming equal credit risk for both alternative***, she gets a better return from her friend's business.

13. Find the Present Value for each Buyer.

Buyer A:

$PV_A = FV(1 + i)^{-n} = FV\left(1 + \frac{r}{1}\right)^{-n} = \$5,000\left(1 + \frac{0.04}{1}\right)^{-1\cdot4} = \$5,000(1.04)^{-4}$

$\quad = \$4,274.02$

Total Present value = \$20,000 + PV_A = \$20,000 + \$4,274.02 = \$24,274.02

Buyer B:

$PV_B = FV(1 + i)^{-n} = FV\left(1 + \frac{r}{1}\right)^{-n} = \$10,000\left(1 + \frac{0.04}{1}\right)^{-1\cdot3} = \$10,000(1.04)^{-3}$

$\quad = \$8,889.96$

Total Present value = \$15,000 + PV_B = \$15,000 + \$8,889.96 = \$23,889.96

Buyer C:

$PV_C = FV(1 + i)^{-n} = FV\left(1 + \frac{r}{1}\right)^{-n} = \$18,000\left(1 + \frac{0.04}{1}\right)^{-1\cdot6} = \$18,000(1.04)^{-6}$

$\quad = \$14,225.66$

Total Present value = \$10,000 + PV_C = \$10,000 + \$14,225.66 = \$24,225.66

Assuming equal credit risk, **Buyer A** has made the best offer with \$24,270.02.

15. **1st Opportunity**:

$\quad PV = FV(1 + i)^{-n} = FV\left(1 + \frac{r}{1}\right)^{-n} = \$8,000\left(1 + \frac{0.06}{1}\right)^{-1\cdot4} = \$8,000(1.06)^{-4}$

$\quad = \$6,336.75$

2nd Opportunity:

$\quad PV = FV(1 + i)^{-n} = FV\left(1 + \frac{r}{1}\right)^{-n} = \$7,000\left(1 + \frac{0.06}{1}\right)^{-1\cdot2} = \$7,000(1.06)^{-2}$

$\quad = \$6,229.98$

3rd Opportunity:

$$PV = FV(1 + i)^{-n} = FV\left(1 + \frac{r}{1}\right)^{-n} = \$10,000\left(1 + \frac{.06}{1}\right)^{-1 \cdot 7} = \$10,000(1.06)^{-7}$$

$$= \$6,650.57$$

Assuming equal credit risk, the 3rd opportunity is best.

17. $FV = (1 + i)^n PV$

$$\frac{FV}{PV} = \frac{(1+i)^n PV}{PV}$$

$$\left(\frac{FV}{PV}\right)^{1/n} = (1 + i)^{n/n} = 1 + i$$

$$\frac{FV}{PV} = \frac{(1+i)^n \cancel{PV}}{\cancel{PV}}$$

$$\left(\frac{FV}{PV}\right)^{1/n} = 1 + i$$

$$\frac{FV}{PV} = (1 + i)^n$$

$$-1 \qquad -1$$

$$\left(\frac{FV}{PV}\right)^{1/n} = [(1 + i)^n]^{1/n}$$

$$\left(\frac{FV}{PV}\right)^{1/n} - 1 = i \quad \text{or} \quad i = \left(\frac{FV}{PV}\right)^{1/n} - 1$$

19. $i = \left(\frac{FV}{PV}\right)^{1/n} - 1 = \left(\frac{1,350}{1,000}\right)^{\frac{1}{3}} - 1 = 1.1052 - 1 = .1052 = 10.52\%$

21. $i = \left(\frac{2x}{x}\right)^{1/10} - 1 = (2)^{0.10} - 1 = 1.0718 - 1 = 0.0718 = 7.18\%$

Section 3.3: Net Present Values of Cash Flows

1. $PV_1 = FV(1 + i)^{-n} = FV\left(1 + \frac{r}{1}\right)^{-n} = \$750\left(1 + \frac{0.02}{1}\right)^{-1 \cdot 1} = \$750(1.02)^{-1}$

$$= \$735.29$$

$PV_2 = FV(1 + i)^{-n} = FV\left(1 + \frac{r}{1}\right)^{-n} = \$1,100\left(1 + \frac{0.02}{1}\right)^{-1 \cdot 2} = \$1,100(1.02)^{-2}$
$$= \$1,057.29$$

$PV_3 = FV(1 + i)^{-n} = FV\left(1 + \frac{r}{1}\right)^{-n} = \$2,000\left(1 + \frac{0.02}{1}\right)^{-1 \cdot 4} = \$2,000(1.02)^{-4}$
$$= \$1,847.69$$

$NPV = (PV_1 + PV_2 + PV_3) - C_0 = \$3,640.27 - \$2,500 = \$1,140.27$

3. $PV_1 = FV(1 + i)^{-n} = FV\left(1 + \frac{r}{12}\right)^{-n} = \$500\left(1 + \frac{0.025}{12}\right)^{-0.5(12)}$

$$= \$500\left(1 + \frac{0.025}{12}\right)^{-6} = \$493.80$$

$$PV_2 = FV(1+i)^{-n} = FV\left(1+\frac{r}{12}\right)^{-n} = \$1{,}000\left(1+\frac{.025}{12}\right)^{-1.25(12)}$$

$$= \$1{,}000\left(1+\frac{0.025}{12}\right)^{-15} = \$969.26$$

$$PV_3 = FV(1+i)^{-n} = FV\left(1+\frac{r}{12}\right)^{-n} = \$2{,}000\left(1+\frac{0.025}{12}\right)^{-3(12)}$$

$$= \$2{,}000\left(1+\frac{0.025}{12}\right)^{-36} = \$1{,}855.63$$

Total Present Value $= PV_1 + PV_2 + PV_3 = \$3{,}318.69$

Net Present Value $= \$3{,}318.69 - \$2{,}900 = \$418.69$

5. **Time saving plan:** $PV = FV(1+i)^{-n} = FV\left(1+\frac{r}{1}\right)^{-n} = \$2{,}000\left(1+\frac{0.05}{1}\right)^{-1\cdot3}$

$$= \$2{,}000(1.05)^{-3} = \$1{,}727.68$$

Lend to friend: $PV_1 = FV(1+i)^{-n} = FV\left(1+\frac{r}{1}\right)^{-n} = \$750\left(1+\frac{0.05}{1}\right)^{-1\cdot1}$

$$= \$750(1.05)^{-1} = \$714.29$$

$$PV_2 = FV(1+i)^{-n} = FV\left(1+\frac{r}{1}\right)^{-n} \$750\left(1+\frac{0.05}{1}\right)^{-1\cdot2}$$

$$= \$750(1.05)^{-2} = \$680.27$$

$$PV_3 = FV(1+i)^{-n} = FV\left(1+\frac{r}{1}\right)^{-n} = \$750\left(1+\frac{0.05}{1}\right)^{-1\cdot3}$$

$$= \$750(1.05)^{-3} = \$647.88$$

Total present value $= PV_1 + PV_2 + PV_3 = \$2{,}042.44$

Assuming equal credit risk, lending the money to a friend is more profitable.

Section 3.4: Ordinary Annuities

1. $PV = R\left[\frac{1-(1+i)^{-n}}{i}\right] = \$50\left[\frac{1-\left(1+\frac{0.04}{4}\right)^{-4\cdot10}}{\frac{0.04}{4}}\right] = \$50\left[\frac{1-(1.01)^{-40}}{.01}\right] = \$1{,}641.73$

3. $PV = R\left[\frac{1-(1+i)^{-n}}{i}\right] = \$750\left[\frac{1-\left(1+\frac{0.08}{1}\right)^{-1\cdot3}}{\frac{0.08}{1}}\right] = \$750\left[\frac{1-(1.08)^{-3}}{.08}\right] = \$1{,}932.82$

$NPV = PV - C_0 = \$1{,}932.82 - \$1{,}500 = \$432.82$

5. **1st Investment:**

$$PV_1 = R\left[\frac{1-(1+i)^{-n}}{i}\right] = \$2{,}000\left[\frac{1-\left(1+\frac{0.04}{12}\right)^{-12\cdot2}}{\frac{0.04}{12}}\right] = \$2{,}000\left[\frac{1-\left(1+\frac{0.04}{12}\right)^{-24}}{\frac{0.04}{12}}\right]$$

$$= \$2{,}000\left(\frac{12}{0.04}\right)\left[1-\left(1+\frac{0.04}{12}\right)^{-24}\right] = \$46{,}056.50$$

$$PV_2 = FV(1+i)^{-n} = \$38{,}000\left(1+\frac{0.04}{12}\right)^{-12\cdot2} = \$38{,}000\left(1+\frac{0.04}{12}\right)^{-24}$$

$$= \$35{,}083.09$$

$$NPV_1 = PV_1 + PV_2 - C_0 = \$46{,}056.50 + \$35{,}083.09 - \$70{,}000$$
$$= \$11{,}139.59$$

2nd Investment:

$$PV = R\left[\frac{1-(1+i)^{-n}}{i}\right] = \$3{,}500\left[\frac{1-\left(1+\frac{0.04}{12}\right)^{-12\cdot2}}{\frac{0.04}{12}}\right] = \$3{,}500\left[\frac{1-\left(1+\frac{0.04}{12}\right)^{-24}}{\frac{0.04}{12}}\right]$$

$$= \$3{,}500\left(\frac{12}{0.04}\right)\left[1-\left(1+\frac{0.04}{12}\right)^{-24}\right] = \$80{,}598.88$$

$$NPV_2 = PV - C_0 = \$80{,}598.88 - \$70{,}000 = \$10{,}598.88$$

On a strictly monetary basis, and assuming equal credit risk for both investments, the first investment is more profitable.

7. **1st Investment:**

$$PV = R\left[\frac{1-(1+i)^{-n}}{i}\right] = \$2{,}300\left[\frac{1-\left(1+\frac{0.04}{4}\right)^{-4\cdot3}}{\frac{0.04}{4}}\right] = \$2{,}300\left[\frac{1-(1+0.01)^{-12}}{0.01}\right]$$

$$= \$25{,}886.68$$

$$NPV_1 = PV - C_0 = \$25{,}886.68 - \$20{,}000 = \$5{,}886.68$$

2nd Investment:

$$PV = R\left[\frac{1-(1+i)^{-n}}{i}\right] = \$1{,}500\left[\frac{1-\left(1+\frac{0.04}{4}\right)^{-4\cdot4}}{\frac{0.04}{4}}\right] = \$1{,}500\left[\frac{1-(1+0.01)^{-16}}{0.01}\right]$$

$$= \$22{,}076.81$$

$$NPV_2 = PV + 2{,}000 - C_0 = \$22{,}076.81 + \$2{,}000 - \$18{,}000 = \$6{,}076.8$$

On a strictly monetary basis, and assuming equal credit risk for both investments, the second investment is more profitable. (Note: to compare investments the same amount must be considered in both NPVs. Thus, in the second alternative, after investing $18,000, there is still $2,000 of intermediate, or Present Value, funds available, which must be added to the NPV.)

9. $PV_1 = R\left[\dfrac{1-(1+i)^{-n}}{i}\right] = \$80\left[\dfrac{1-\left(1+\frac{0.06}{2}\right)^{-20}}{\frac{0.06}{2}}\right] = \$80\left[\dfrac{1-(1+0.03)^{-20}}{0.03}\right] = \$1,190.20$

$PV_2 = \$1,000\left(1+\dfrac{0.06}{2}\right)^{-20} = \$1,000(1+0.03)^{-20} = \$553.68$

Total Present value $= PV_1 + PV_2 = \$1,190.20 + \$553.68 = \$1,743.88$

11. $FV = R\left[\dfrac{(1+i)^n-1}{i}\right] = \$40\left[\dfrac{\left(1+\frac{0.04}{4}\right)^{4\cdot3}-1}{\frac{0.04}{4}}\right] = \$400\left[\dfrac{(1+0.01)^{12}-1}{0.01}\right]$

$= \$400\left[\dfrac{(1.01)^{12}-1}{.01}\right] = \$5,073.00$

13. $FV = R\left[\dfrac{(1+i)^n-1}{i}\right] = \$20\left[\dfrac{\left(1+\frac{0.05}{52}\right)^{52\cdot\frac{48}{52}}-1}{\frac{0.05}{52}}\right]$

$= \$20\left(\dfrac{52}{0.05}\right)\left[\left(1+\dfrac{0.05}{52}\right)^{48}-1\right] = \$982.02$

Section 3.5: Mortgages and Amortization Tables

1. $R = \dfrac{PV}{\left[\frac{1-(1+i)^{-n}}{i}\right]} = \dfrac{\$36,000}{\left[\frac{1-\left(1+\frac{0.04}{12}\right)^{-30\cdot12}}{\frac{0.04}{12}}\right]} = \dfrac{\$36,000}{\left[\frac{1-\left(1+\frac{0.04}{12}\right)^{-360}}{\frac{0.04}{12}}\right]} = \dfrac{\$36,000}{\left[\frac{.6982041}{\frac{0.04}{12}}\right]}$

$= \dfrac{\$36,000}{209.4612404} = \$171.87$

3. Total Interest Paid $= (R\cdot n) - PV = (\$171.87\cdot12\cdot30) - \$36,000$

$= \$61,873.20 - \$36,000 = \$25,873.20$

5. **See Figure 3.9 Column D in the textbook**

Total Interest Paid

= $4.17 + $3.83 +$3.49 + $3.14 + $2.80 +$2.46 + $2.11 + $1.76 + $1.41+ $1.06 + $0.71 + $0.36
= $27.30

See Equation 3.17 in the textbook

Total Interest Paid $= (R \cdot n) - PV = (\$85.61 \cdot 1 \cdot 12) - \$1,000 = \$27.32^*$

* The two answers are slightly different due to rounding.

7. (a) $R = \dfrac{PV}{\left[\dfrac{1-(1+i)^{-n}}{i}\right]} = \dfrac{\$45,000}{\left[\dfrac{1-\left(1+\frac{0.04}{12}\right)^{-4\cdot12}}{\frac{0.04}{12}}\right]} = \dfrac{\$45,000}{\left[\dfrac{1-\left(1+\frac{0.04}{12}\right)^{-48}}{\frac{0.04}{12}}\right]} = \dfrac{\$45,000}{\left[\dfrac{0.1476294}{\frac{0.04}{12}}\right]}$

$= \dfrac{\$45,000}{44.28882} = \$1,016.06$

(b) Total Interest Paid $= (R \cdot n) - PV = (\$1,016.06 \cdot 12 \cdot 4) - \$45,000$

$= \$48,770.88 - \$45,000 = \$3,770.88$

(c) **Payment 1**:

Interest Paid $= I_1 = (\$45,000)\left(\frac{0.04}{12}\right) = \$150$

Principal Paid $= Monthly\ Payment - Interest\ Paid = \$1,016.06 - \$150 = \$866.06$

Outstanding Balance $= \$45,000 - Principal\ Paid = \$45,000 - \$866.06 = \$44,133.94$

Payment 2:

Interest Paid $= I_2 = (\$44,133.94)\left(\frac{0.04}{12}\right) = \$147.11$

Principal Paid $= Monthly\ Payment - Interest\ Paid = \$1,016.06 - \$147.11 = \$868.95$

Outstanding Balance $= \$45,000 - Principal\ Paid = \$44,133.94 - \$868.95 = \$43,264.99$

Payment 3:

Interest Paid $= I_3 = (\$43,264.99)\left(\frac{0.04}{12}\right) = \$144.22$

Principal Paid $= Monthly\ Payment - Interest\ Paid = \$1,016.06 - \$144.2 = \$871.84$

Outstanding Balance $= \$43,264.99 - Principal\ Paid = \$43,264.99 - \$871.84 = \$42,393.15$

	A	B	C	D	E	F	G
1	Amount of Loan:	$45,000					
2	Length of Loan (in years):	4					
3	Annual Interest Rate:	4%					
4	Monthly Payment:	$1,016.06					
5							
6			Payment Number	Payment Amount	Interest Paid	Principal Paid	Outstanding Balance
7			0	-	-	-	$45,000.00
8			1	$1,016.06	$150.00	$866.06	$44,133.94
9			2	$1,016.06	$147.11	$868.95	$43,264.99
10			3	$1,016.06	$144.22	$871.84	$42,393.15

9. Monthly Payment:

$$R = \frac{PV}{\left[\frac{1-(1+i)^{-n}}{i}\right]} = \frac{\$800}{\left[\frac{1-\left(1+\frac{0.04}{12}\right)^{-1\cdot12}}{\frac{0.04}{12}}\right]} = \frac{\$800}{\left[\frac{1-\left(1+\frac{0.04}{12}\right)^{-12}}{\frac{0.04}{12}}\right]} = \frac{\$800}{\left[\frac{.039146648}{\frac{0.04}{12}}\right]}$$

$$= \frac{\$800}{11.7439944} = \$68.12$$

Payment 1:

Interest Paid $= I_1 = (\$800)\left(\frac{0.04}{12}\right) = \$2.67$

Principal Paid $= Monthly\ Payment - Interest\ Paid = \$68.12 - \$2.67 = \$65.45$

Outstanding Balance $= \$800 - Principal\ Paid = \$800 - \$65.45 = \$734.55$

Payment 2:

Interest Paid $= I_2 = (\$734.55)\left(\frac{0.04}{12}\right) = \$2.45$

Principal Paid $= Monthly\ Payment - Interest\ Paid = \$68.12 - \$2.45 = \$65.67$

Outstanding Balance $= \$734.55 - Principal\ Paid = \$734.55 - \$65.67 = \$668.88$

Payment 3:

Interest Paid $= I_3 = (\$668.88)\left(\frac{0.04}{12}\right) = \$2.23$

Principal Paid $= Monthly\ Payment - Interest\ Paid = \$68.12 - \$2.23 = \$65.89$

Outstanding Balance $= \$668.88 - Principal\ Paid = \$668.88 - \$65.89 = \$602.99$

Payment 4:

Interest Paid $= I_4 = (\$602.99)\left(\frac{0.04}{12}\right) = \$2.01$

Principal Paid $= Monthly\ Payment - Interest\ Paid = \$68.12 - \$2.01 = \$66.11$

Outstanding Balance $= \$602.99 - Principal\ Paid = \$602.99 - \$66.11 = \$536.88$

Payment 5:

Interest Paid $= I_5 = (\$536.88)\left(\frac{0.04}{12}\right) = \$1.79$

Principal Paid $= Monthly\ Payment - Interest\ Paid = \$68.12 - \$1.79 = \$66.33$

Outstanding Balance $= \$536.88 - Principal\ Paid = \$536.88 - \$66.33 = \$470.55$

Payment 6:

Interest Paid $= I_6 = (\$470.55)\left(\frac{0.04}{12}\right) = \$1.57$

Principal Paid $= Monthly\ Payment - Interest\ Paid = \$68.12 - \$1.57 = \$66.55$

Outstanding Balance $= \$470.55 - Principal\ Paid = \$470.55 - \$66.55 = \$404.00$

Payment 7:

Interest Paid $= I_7 = (\$404)\left(\frac{0.04}{12}\right) = \$1.35$

Principal Paid $= Monthly\ Payment - Interest\ Paid = \$68.12 - \$1.35 = \$66.77$

Outstanding Balance $= \$404 - Principal\ Paid = \$404 - \$66.77 = \$337.23$

Payment 8:

Interest Paid $= I_8 = (\$337.23)\left(\frac{0.04}{12}\right) = \$1.12$

Principal Paid $= Monthly\ Payment - Interest\ Paid = \$68.12 - \$1.12 = \$67.00$

Outstanding Balance $= \$337.23 - Principal\ Paid = \$337.23 - \$67.00 = \$270.23$

Payment 9:

Interest Paid $= I_9 = (\$270.23)\left(\frac{0.04}{12}\right) = \$0.90$

Principal Paid $= Monthly\ Payment - Interest\ Paid = \$68.12 - \$0.90 = \$67.22$

Outstanding Balance $= \$270.23 - Principal\ Paid = \$270.23 - \$67.22 = \$203.01$

Payment 10:

Interest Paid $= I_{10} = (\$203.01)\left(\frac{0.04}{12}\right) = \$0.68$

Principal Paid $= Monthly\ Payment - Interest\ Paid = \$68.12 - \$0.68 = \$67.44$

Outstanding Balance $= \$203.01 - Principal\ Paid = \$203.01 - \$67.44 = \$135.57$

Payment 11:

Interest Paid $= I_{11} = (\$135.57)\left(\frac{0.04}{12}\right) = \$0.45$

Principal Paid $= Monthly\ Payment - Interest\ Paid = \$68.12 - \$0.45 = \$67.67$

Outstanding Balance $= \$135.57 - Principal\ Paid = \$135.57 - \$67.67 = \$67.90$

Payment 12:

Interest Paid $= I_{12} = (\$67.90)\left(\frac{0.04}{12}\right) = \$0.23$

Principal Paid $= Monthly\ Payment - Interest\ Paid = \$68.12 - \$0.23 = \$67.89.$

Because of rounding, the last payment should be \$67.90 instead of 67.89 as calculated.

Outstanding Balance $= 0$

	A	B	C	D	E	F	G
1	Amount of Loan:	$800					
2	Length of Loan (in years):	1					
3	Annual Interest Rate:	4%					
4	Monthly Payment:	$68.12					
5							
6			Payment Number	Payment Amount	Interest Paid	Principal Paid	Outstanding Balance
7			0	-	-	-	$800.00
8			1	$68.12	$2.67	$65.45	$734.55
9			2	$68.12	$2.45	$65.67	$668.88
10			3	$68.12	$2.23	$65.89	$602.99
11			4	$68.12	$2.01	$66.11	$536.88
12			5	$68.12	$1.79	$66.33	$470.55
13			6	$68.12	$1.57	$66.55	$404.00
14			7	$68.12	$1.35	$66.77	$337.23
15			8	$68.12	$1.12	$67.00	$270.23
16			9	$68.12	$0.90	$67.22	$203.01
17			10	$68.12	$0.68	$67.44	$135.57
18			11	$68.12	$0.45	$67.67	$67.90
19			12	$68.12	$0.23	$67.90	$0.00

Section 3.6: Installment Loans and Interest Charges

1. (a) Total Interest Charge = $(0.08)(\$3,000)(2) = \$480$

   $$\text{Monthly installment payment} = \frac{\$480 + \$3,000}{12(2)} = \frac{\$3,480}{24} = \$145.00$$

   (b) Total Interest Charge = $(0.08)(\$3,000)(3) = \$720.00$

   $$\text{Monthly installment payment} = \frac{\$720 + \$3,000}{12(3)} = \frac{\$3,720}{36} = \$103.33$$

   (c) 14.677% for the 2 year loan; 14.546% for the 3 year loan.

3. (a) Total Interest Charge = $(0.06)(\$4,000)(1) = \$240$

   (b) Monthly installment payment $= \dfrac{\$240 + \$4,000}{12(1)} = \dfrac{\$4,240}{12} = \$353.33$

   (c) For Present Value of $4,000, a payment of $353.33 for 12 months (1 year), the true interest rate is 10.895%.

5. (a) Monthly payment $= \dfrac{\$9,000}{12(3)} = \dfrac{\$9,000}{36} = \$250$

   (c) Total Interest Charged = $(0.06)(\$9,000)(3) = \$1,620.00$

   (d) Cash Received = Amount of loan – Total interest Charged = $9,000 – $1,620 = $7,380

   (e) For a Present Value of $7,380, a payment of $250 for 36 months, the true interest is 13.376%.

7. (a) $Amount\ of\ loan = \dfrac{cash\ Received}{1-rt} = \dfrac{\$15,000}{1-(0.04)(5)} = \dfrac{\$15,000}{0.8} = \$18,750$

   (b) $R = \dfrac{Amount\ of\ Loan}{Length\ of\ loan, in\ months} = \dfrac{\$18,750}{12(5)} = \dfrac{\$18,750}{60} = \$312.50$

   (c) Total interest charged = $18,750 – $15,000 = $3,750

   (d) For a Present Value of $15,000, a payment of $312.50 for 60 months (5 years), the true interest rate is 9.154%.

Section 3.7: Annuities Due

1. $PV = R + R\left[\frac{1-(1+i)^{-(n-1)}}{i}\right] = \$1{,}000 + \$1{,}000\left[\frac{1-\left(1+\frac{0.04}{1}\right)^{-(10\cdot1-1)}}{\frac{0.04}{1}}\right]$

$\quad = \$1{,}000 + \$1{,}000\left[\frac{1-(1+0.04)^{-9}}{0.04}\right] = \$1{,}000 + \$1{,}000(7.435332)$

$\quad = \$1{,}000 + \$7{,}435.33 = \$8{,}435.33$

3. $PV = R + R\left[\frac{1-(1+i)^{-(n-1)}}{i}\right] = \$20 + \$20\left[\frac{1-\left(1+\frac{0.02}{12}\right)^{-(15\cdot12-1)}}{\frac{0.02}{12}}\right]$

$\quad = \$20 + \$20\left[\frac{1-\left(1+\frac{0.02}{12}\right)^{-179}}{\frac{0.02}{12}}\right] = \$20 + \$20\left[\frac{0.2577618}{0.0016667}\right]$

$\quad = \$20 + \$20(154.6539869) = \$20 + \$3{,}093.08 = \$3{,}113.80$

5. $FV = R\left[\frac{(1+i)^{(n+1)}-1}{i}\right] - R = \$40\left[\frac{\left(1+\frac{0.04}{4}\right)^{(4\cdot3+1)}-1}{\frac{0.04}{4}}\right] - \$40$

$\quad = \$40\left[\frac{(1+0.01)^{13}-1}{0.01}\right] - \$40 = \$40(13.8093280) - \$40$

$\quad = \$552.37 - \$40 = \$512.37$

7. $FV = R\left[\frac{(1+i)^{(n+1)}-1}{i}\right] - R = \$20\left[\frac{\left(1+\frac{0.05}{52}\right)^{\left(52\cdot\frac{48}{52}+1\right)}-1}{\frac{0.05}{52}}\right] - \$20$

$\quad = \$20\left[\frac{\left(1+\frac{.05}{52}\right)^{(48+1)}}{\frac{.05}{52}}\right] - \$20 = \$20\left[\frac{\left(1+\frac{.05}{52}\right)^{49}-1}{\frac{.05}{52}}\right] - \$20$

$\quad = \$20\left[\frac{0.0482192}{0.0009615}\right] - \$20 = \$20(50.149974) - \$20$

$\quad = \$1{,}003 - \$20 = \$983.00$

9. $FV = R\left[\frac{(1+i)^{(n+1)}-1}{i}\right] - R = \$1\left[\frac{\left(1+\frac{0.05}{365}\right)^{(365\cdot2+1)}-1}{\frac{0.05}{365}}\right] - \$1$

$= \$1\left[\frac{\left(1+\frac{0.05}{365}\right)^{731}-1}{\frac{0.05}{365}}\right] - \$1 = \$1\left[\frac{0.1053147}{0.000137}\right] - \$1 = \$1(768.72) - \$1$

$= \$768.72 - \$1 = \$767.72$

11. $FV = R\left[\frac{(1+i)^{(n+1)}-1}{i}\right] - R = \$1,000\left[\frac{\left(1+\frac{0.08}{1}\right)^{(1\cdot7+1)}-1}{\frac{0.08}{1}}\right] - \$1,000$

$= \$1,000\left[\frac{(1.08)^8-1}{0.08}\right] - \$1,000 = \$1,000(10.636628) - \$1,000$

$= \$10,636.63 - \$1,000 = \$9,636.63$

Section 3.8: Effective Interest Rate

1. $E = (1+i)^n - 1 = \left(1+\frac{0.02}{4}\right)^4 - 1 = (1.005)^4 - 1 = 0.020151 = 2.0151\%$

3. $E_c = e^i - 1 = e^{0.02} - 1 = 0.020201 = 2.0201\%$

5. $E_c = e^i - 1 = e^{0.04} - 1 = 0.040811 = 4.0811\%$

7. $E = (1+i)^n - 1 = \left(1+\frac{0.08}{4}\right)^4 - 1 = (1.02)^4 - 1 = 0.0824322 = 8.2432\%$

Chapter 4 Rates of Change: The Derivative

Section 4.1: Concept of a Function

1. The relation defines a function, because each element in the first set is assigned to only one element in the second set.

3. The relation does not define a function, because the element *a* in the first set is assigned to two elements, *A* and *B*, in the second set.

5. The relation defines a function, because each element in the first set is assigned to only one element in the second set.

7. The relation does not define a function, because the element *b* in the first set is is not assigned to any element in the second set.

9. The relation defines a function, because each element in the first set is assigned to only one element in the second set.

11. The relation defines a function, because each element in the first set is assigned to only one element in the second set.

13. The relation defines a function, because each element in the first set is assigned to only one element in the second set. No *x* component repeats.

15. (a) The relation defines a function, because each student has only one height measurement.

    (b) The relation defines a function, because each student has only one name.

    (c) The relation does not define a function, because a name could belong to more than one student.

    (d) The relation defines a function, because each stock that is listed on the New York Exchange has only one closing price.

    (e) The relation does not define a function, because a closing stock price might be the same for more than one stock listed on the New York Stock Exchange.

    (f) The relation does not define a function, because each car might have more than one color painted on it.

    (g) The relation does not define a function, because the same rate might be offered at more than bank.

Section 4.2: Mathematical Functions

1. (a) Domain = {0, 1, 2, 3, 4, 5, 6, 7, 8, 9, 10}

   (b) To find the range of the function, evaluate the function at each z-value in Part (a). We have:

   For $z = 0, D = (0)^2 - 30(0) + 225 = 225$

   For $z = 1, D = (1)^2 - 30(1) + 225 = 196$

   For $z = 2, D = (2)^2 - 30(2) + 225 = 4 - 60 + 225 = 169$

   For $z = 3, D = (3)^2 - 30(3) + 225 = 9 - 90 + 225 = 144$

   For $z = 4, D = (4)^2 - 30(4) + 225 = 16 - 120 + 225 = 121$

   For $z = 5, D = (5)^2 - 30(5) + 225 = 25 - 150 + 225 = 100$

   For $z = 6, D = (6)^2 - 30(6) + 225 = 36 - 180 + 225 = 81$

   For $z = 7, D = (7)^2 - 30(7) + 225 = 49 - 210 + 225 = 64$

   For $z = 8, D = (8)^2 - 30(8) + 225 = 64 - 240 + 225 = 49$

   For $z = 9, D = (9)^2 - 30(9) + 225 = 81 - 270 + 225 = 36$

   For $z = 10, D = (10)^2 - 30(10) + 225 = 100 - 300 + 225 = 25$

   Range = {225, 196, 169, 144, 121, 100, 81, 64, 49, 36, 25}

3. $y = 2 + 3x$ is a linear equation. This means, for every x in the domain, there will be one and only one corresponding y in the range. As a matter of fact, for every unique x in the domain, there corresponds a unique y in the range. Therefore, $y = 2 + 3x$ is a function of x.

   Since $y = 2 + 3x$ is also a one-to-one function, it has an inverse function. To find the inverse of a one-to-one function, solve the given equation for x.

   $$2 + 3x = y$$
   $$\underline{-2 \qquad -2}$$
   $$3x = y - 2$$
   $$\frac{3x}{3} = \frac{y-2}{3}$$

   $$x = \frac{y-2}{3} = \frac{y}{3} - \frac{2}{3}$$
   $$x = \frac{1}{3}y - \frac{2}{3}$$

   This is a linear relationship where each y in $0 \le y < \infty$. There is one x *for each y.*

5. $z = 2w^2 + 4$ is a quadratic relationship, where each w in the domain has only one z in the range. Therefore, $z = 2w^2 + 4$ is a function of w.

Since $z = 2w^2 + 4$ is not a one-to-one function, it does not have an inverse that is a function. To verify this, solve the equation for w. We have:

$$z = 2w^2 + 4$$

$$2w^2 + 4 = z$$

$$\underline{-4 \quad -4}$$

$$2w^2 = z - 4$$

$$\frac{2w^2}{2} = \frac{z-4}{2}$$

$$w^2 = \frac{z-4}{2}$$

$$(w^2)^{1/2} = \pm\left(\frac{z-4}{2}\right)^{1/2}$$

$$w = \pm\sqrt{\frac{z-4}{2}}$$

The inverse relation is not a function, because for every z in $4 \le z \le 10$, there corresponds two values of w.

7. (a) $f(2) = (2)^2 + 3(2) - 6 = 4 + 6 - 6 = 4$

(b) $f(5) = (5)^2 + 3(5) - 6 = 25 + 15 - 6 = 34$

(c) $f(0) = (0)^2 + 3(0) - 6 = 0 + 0 - 6 = -6$

(d) $f(a + b) = (a + b)^2 + 3(a + b) - 6 = (a + b)(a + b) + 3(a + b) - 6$

$$= a^2 + ab + ba + b^2 + 3a + 3b - 6$$

$$= a^2 + ab + ab + b^2 + 3a + 3b - 6$$

$$= a^2 + 2ab + b^2 + 3a + 3b - 6$$

(e) $f(x + \Delta x) = (x + \Delta x)^2 + 3(x + \Delta x) - 6 = (x + \Delta x)(x + \Delta x) + 3(x + \Delta x) - 6$

$$= x^2 + x(\Delta x) + (\Delta x)x + 3x + 3\Delta x - 6$$

$$= x^2 + x(\Delta x) + x(\Delta x) + (\Delta x)^2 + 3x + 3(\Delta x) - 6$$

$$= x^2 + 3x - 6 + 2x(\Delta x) + 3(\Delta x) + (\Delta x)^2$$

9. (a) $f(2) = 2 + 2(2)^2 + (2)^3 = 2 + 8 + 8 = 18$

(b) $f(d) = d + 2(d)^2 + (d)^3 = d + 2d^2 + d^3$

(c) $f(x + y) = (x + y) + 2(x + y)^2 + (x + y)^3 = x + y + 2(x + y)^2 + (x + y)^3$

(d) $f(2a) = 2a + 2(2a)^2 + (2a)^3 = 2a + 2(4a^2) + 8a^3 = 2a + 8a^2 + 8a^3$

Section 4.3: Average Rate of Change

1. For problems (a) – (d), the average rate of change in y with respect to x over $[x_1, x_2]$

$$= \frac{f(x_2) - f(x_1)}{x_2 - x_1}.$$

(a) $f(x_1) = f(1) = (1)^2 - 4(1) + 5 = 1 - 4 + 5 = 2$

$f(x_2) = f(10) = (10)^2 - 4(10) + 5 = 100 - 40 + 5 = 65$

The average rate of change $= \dfrac{f(x_2) - f(x_1)}{x_2 - x_1} = \dfrac{65 - 2}{10 - 1} = \dfrac{63}{9} = 7$

(b) $f(x_1) = f(1) = (1)^2 - 4(1) + 5 = 1 - 4 + 5 = 2$

$f(x_2) = f(8) = (8)^2 - 4(8) + 5 = 64 - 32 + 5 = 37$

The average rate of change $= \dfrac{f(x_2) - f(x_1)}{x_2 - x_1} = \dfrac{37 - 2}{8 - 1} = \dfrac{35}{7} = 5$

(c) $f(x_1) = f(-2) = (-2)^2 - 4(-2) + 5 = 4 + 8 + 5 = 17$

$f(x_2) = f(1) = (1)^2 - 4(1) + 5 = 1 - 4 + 5 = 2$

The average rate of change $= \dfrac{f(x_2) - f(x_1)}{x_2 - x_1} = \dfrac{2 - 17}{1 - (-2)} = \dfrac{-15}{1 + 2} = \dfrac{-15}{3} = -5$

(d) $f(x_1) = f(-3) = (-3)^2 - 4(-3) + 5 = 9 + 12 + 5 = 26$

$f(x_2) = f(-1) = (-1)^2 - 4(-1) + 5 = 1 + 4 + 5 = 10$

The average rate of change $= \dfrac{f(x_2) - f(x_1)}{x_2 - x_1} = \dfrac{10 - 26}{-1 - (-3)} = \dfrac{-16}{-1 + 3} = \dfrac{-16}{2} = -8$

3. (a) $f(x_1) = f(1) = 3(1) - 4 = 3 - 4 = -1$

$f(x_2) = f(5) = 3(5) - 4 = 15 - 4 = 11$

The average rate of change $= \dfrac{f(x_2) - f(x_1)}{x_2 - x_1} = \dfrac{11 - (-1)}{5 - 1} = \dfrac{11 + 1}{4} = \dfrac{12}{4} = 3$

(b) $f(x_1) = f(1) = (1)^2 + 6(1) + 2 = 1 + 6 + 2 = 9$

$f(x_2) = f(5) = (5)^2 + 6(5) + 2 = 25 + 30 + 2 = 5$

The average rate of change $= \dfrac{f(x_2) - f(x_1)}{x_2 - x_1} = \dfrac{57 - 9}{5 - 1} = \dfrac{48}{4} = 12$

(c) $y(x_1) = y(1) = (1)^3 + 5 = 1 + 5 = 6$

$y(x_2) = y(5) = (5)^3 + 5 = 125 + 5 = 130$

The average rate of change $= \dfrac{y(x_2) - y(x_1)}{x_2 - x_1} = \dfrac{130 - 6}{5 - 1} = \dfrac{124}{4} = 31$

(d) $s(t_1) = s(1) = 2 - 3(1)^2 = 2 - 3 = -1$

$s(t_2) = s(5) = 2 - 3(5)^2 - 3(25) = 2 - 75 = -73$

The average rate of change $= \dfrac{s(t_2) - s(t_1)}{t_2 - t_1} = \dfrac{-73 - (-1)}{5 - 1} = \dfrac{-73 + 1}{4} = \dfrac{-72}{4} = -18$

5. The average rate of change in y with respect to x over $[x_1, x_2]$

$$= \dfrac{y_2 - y_1}{x_2 - x_1} = \dfrac{\dfrac{1}{x_2} - \dfrac{1}{x_1}}{x_2 - x_1}$$

$$= \dfrac{\dfrac{1}{x_2} \cdot \dfrac{x_1}{x_1} - \dfrac{1}{x_1} \cdot \dfrac{x_2}{x_2}}{x_2 - x_1} = \dfrac{\dfrac{x_1}{x_1 x_2} - \dfrac{x_2}{x_1 x_2}}{x_2 - x_1} = \dfrac{\dfrac{x_1 - x_2}{x_1 x_2}}{x_2 - x_1} = \dfrac{x_1 - x_2}{x_1 x_2} \div \dfrac{(x_2 - x_1)}{1}$$

$$= \dfrac{x_1 - x_2}{x_1 x_2} \cdot \dfrac{1}{x_2 - x_1} = \dfrac{-(x_2 - x_1)}{x_1 x_2} \cdot \dfrac{1}{x_2 - x_1} = \dfrac{-1}{x_1 x_2}, \quad x_1 \neq x_2$$

(a) The average rate of change on $[4, 6] = \dfrac{-1}{x_1 x_2} = \dfrac{-1}{4(6)} = -\dfrac{1}{24} = -0.04167$

(b) The average rate of change on $[3, 7] = \dfrac{-1}{x_1 x_2} = \dfrac{-1}{3(7)} = -\dfrac{1}{21} = -0.04762$

(c) The average rate of change on $[2, 4] = \dfrac{-1}{x_1 x_2} = \dfrac{-1}{2(4)} = -\dfrac{1}{8} = -0.125$

Section 4.4: Instantaneous Rates of Change

1. $m =$ **The slope of a tangent line to the curve defined by the function $f(x)$ at (x, y)**

   $=$ **instantaneous rate of change of $f(x)$ at $x = \displaystyle\lim_{h \to 0} \dfrac{f(x+h) - f(x)}{h}$.**

   (a) First, find the slope of the tangent line to the curve defined by $f(x)$ at (x, y).

   The slope of the tangent line to the curve defined by the function $f(x) = x^2 - 6x + 10$ at $(1, 5) =$ instantaneous rate of change of $f(x) = x^2 - 6x + 10$ at $x = 1$:

$$m = \lim_{h \to 0} \frac{f(1+h) - f(1)}{h}$$

$$m = \lim_{h \to 0} \frac{f(1+h) - f(1)}{h} = \lim_{h \to 0} \frac{\left[(1+h)^2 - 6(1+h) + 10\right] - \left(1^2 - 6(1) + 10\right)}{h}$$

$$= \lim_{h \to 0} \frac{1 + 2h + h^2 - 6 - 6h + 10 - 1 + 6 - 10}{h} = \lim_{h \to 0} \frac{-4h + h^2}{h} = \lim_{h \to 0} \frac{h(-4+h)}{h} = \lim_{h \to 0}(-4 + h) = -4$$

To graph the tangent line to the curve at (1, 5), we will need to find its equation: $y = mx + b$. With $m = -4$, $y = -4x + b$. Use (1, 5) to find b. We have:

$$5 = -4(1) + b$$
$$5 = -4 + b$$
$$+4 \qquad +4$$

$$b = 9$$

The tangent line to the curve at (1, 5) is $y = -4x + 9$.

x	$y = x^2 - 6x + 10$	$y = -4x + 9$
-3	37	21
-2	26	17
-1	17	13
0	10	9
0.5	7.25	7
0.55	7.0025	6.8
0.65	6.5225	6.4
0.75	6.0625	6
1	5	5
2	2	1
3	1	-3
5	5	-11
6	10	-15
7	17	-19
8	26	-23

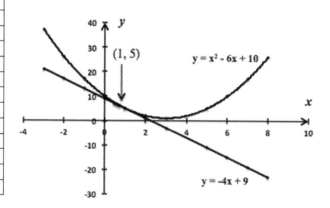

(b) First, find the slope of the tangent line to the curve defined by $f(x)$ at (x, y).

The slope of the tangent line to the curve defined by the function $f(x) = x^2 - 6x + 10$ at $(3,1)$ = instantaneous rate of change of $f(x) = x^2 - 6x + 10$ at $x = 3$:

$$m = \lim_{h \to 0} \frac{f(3+h) - f(3)}{h}.$$

$$m = \lim_{h \to 0} \frac{f(3+h) - f(3)}{h} = \lim_{h \to 0} \frac{\left[(3+h)^2 - 6(3+h) + 10\right] - \left(3^2 - 6(3) + 10\right)}{h}$$

$$= \lim_{h \to 0} \frac{9+6h+h^2-18-6h+10-9+18-10}{h} = \lim_{h \to 0} \frac{h^2}{h} = \lim_{h \to 0} \frac{\cancel{h} \cdot h}{\cancel{h}} = \lim_{h \to 0} h = 0.$$

To graph the tangent line to the curve at (3,1), we will need to find its equation: $y = mx + b$. With $m = 0$, $y = b$. Use (3,1) to find b. We have $1 = b$. The tangent line to the curve at (3,1) is $y = 1$.

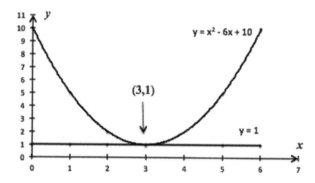

(c) First, find the slope of the tangent line to the curve defined by $f(x)$ at (x, y).

The slope of the tangent line to the curve defined by the function $f(x) = x^2 - 6x + 10$ at $(5, 5)$ = instantaneous rate of change of $f(x) = x^2 - 6x + 10$ at $x = 5$

$$m = \lim_{h \to 0} \frac{f(5+h) - f(5)}{h} = \lim_{h \to 0} \frac{\left[(5+h)^2 - 6(5+h) + 10\right] - \left[5^2 - 6(5) + 10\right]}{h}$$

$$= \lim_{h \to 0} \frac{25+10h+h^2-30-6h+10-25+30-10}{h} = \lim_{h \to 0} \frac{4h+h^2}{h} = \lim_{h \to 0} \frac{\cancel{h}(4+h)}{\cancel{h}} = \lim_{h \to 0}(4+h) = 4$$

To graph the tangent line to the curve at (5,5), we will need to find its equation: $y = mx + b$. With $m = 4$, use (5, 5) to find b. We have:

$$5 = 4(5) + b$$
$$5 = 20 + b$$
$$-20 \quad -20$$
$$b = -15$$

The tangent line to the curve at (5, 5) is $y = 4x - 15$.

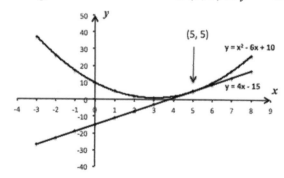

3. (a) To graph the equation, choose arbitrary x-values and then, substitute each x-value into the equation to find its corresponding y-value. Then plot the points on a graph. We have:

For $x = -4$, $y = (-4)^2 + (-4) = 16 - 4 = 12$

For $x = -3$, $y = (-3)^2 + (-3) = 9 - 3 = 6$

For $x = -2$, $y = (-2)^2 + (-2) = 4 - 2 = 2$

For $x = -1$, $y = (-1)^2 + (-1) = 1 - 1 = 0$

For $x = 0$, $\quad y = 0^2 + 0 = 0$

For $x = 1$, $\quad y = (1)^2 + 1 = 1 + 1 = 2$

For $x = 2$, $\quad y = (2)^2 + 2 = 4 + 2 = 6$

For $x = 3$, $\quad y = (3)^2 + 3 = 9 + 3 = 12$

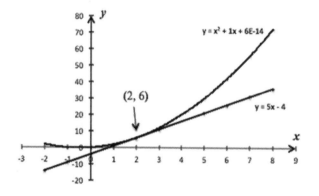

x	$y = x^2 + x$	(x, y)
-4	12	$(-4, 12)$
-3	6	$(-3, 6)$
-2	2	$(-2, 2)$
-1	0	$(-1, 0)$
0	0	$(0, 0)$
1	2	$(1, 2)$
2	6	$(2, 6)$
3	12	$(3, 12)$

(b) For $x_2 = 5.0$, $y_2 = (5.0)^2 + 5.0 = 25 + 5 = 30$

$$\frac{y_2 - y_1}{x_2 - x_1} = \frac{30 - 6}{5.0 - 2} = \frac{24}{3} = 8$$

For $x_2 = 3.0$, $y_2 = (3.0)^2 + 3.0 = 9 + 3.0 = 1$

$$\frac{y_2 - y_1}{x_2 - x_1} = \frac{12 - 6}{3.0 - 2} = \frac{6}{1} = 6$$

For $x_2 = 2.5$, $y_2 = (2.5)^2 + 2.5 = 6.25 + 2.5 = 8.75$

$$\frac{y_2 - y_1}{x_2 - x_1} = \frac{8.75 - 6}{2.5 - 2} = \frac{2.75}{.5} = 5.5$$

For $x_2 = 2.2$, $y_2 = (2.2)^2 + 2.2 = 4.84 + 2.2 = 7.04$

$$\frac{y_2 - y_1}{x_2 - x_1} = \frac{7.04 - 6}{2.2 - 2} = \frac{1.04}{.2} = 5.2$$

For $x_2 = 2.1$, $y_2 = (2.1)^2 + 2.1 = 4.41 + 2.1 = 6.5$

$$\frac{y_2-y_1}{x_2-x_1} = \frac{6.51-6}{2.1-2} = \frac{.51}{.1} = 5.1$$

x_1	x_2	y_1	y_2	$Average\ rate = \dfrac{y_2-y_1}{x_2-x_1}$
2	5.0	6	30	8
2	3.0	6	12	6
2	2.5	6	8.75	5.5
2	2.2	6	7.04	5.2
2	2.1	6	6.51	5.1

Yes. The slope of the tangent line to the curve $y = x^2 + x$ at (2, 6) is 5.

(c) Instantaneous rate of change in $f(x)$ at any $(x, y) = m = \lim\limits_{h \to 0} \dfrac{f(x+h)-f(x)}{h}$.

$$m = \lim\limits_{h \to 0} \frac{f(2+h)-f(2)}{h} = \lim\limits_{h \to 0} \frac{\left[(2+h)^2 + (2+h)\right]-(2^2+2)}{h} = \lim\limits_{h \to 0} \frac{4+4h+h^2+2+h-4-2}{h}$$

$$= \lim\limits_{h \to 0} \frac{5h+h^2}{h} = \lim\limits_{h \to 0} \frac{\cancel{h}(5+h)}{\cancel{h}} = \lim\limits_{h \to 0}(5+h) = 5+0 = 5$$

5. Instantaneous rate of change in $f(x)$ at any $(x, y) = \lim\limits_{h \to 0} \dfrac{f(x+h)-f(x)}{h}$.

$$\lim\limits_{h \to 0} \frac{f(x+h)-f(x)}{h} = \lim\limits_{h \to 0} \frac{2-3(x+h)-(2-3x)}{h} = \lim\limits_{h \to 0} \frac{2-3x-3h-2+3x}{h}$$

$$= \lim\limits_{h \to 0} \frac{-3h}{h} = \lim\limits_{h \to 0} \frac{-3\cancel{h}}{\cancel{h}} = \lim\limits_{h \to 0}(-3) = -3.$$

The instantaneous rate of change at $x = 1$ is -3.

The instantaneous rate of change at $x = -5$ is -3.

7. Instantaneous rate of change in $f(x)$ at any $x = \lim\limits_{h \to 0} \dfrac{f(x+h)-f(x)}{h}$.

$$= \lim\limits_{h \to 0} \frac{f(x+h)-f(x)}{h} = \lim\limits_{h \to 0} \frac{\left[(x+h)^2 - 2(x+h)+10\right]-\left(x^2-2x+10\right)}{h}$$

$$= \lim\limits_{h \to 0} \frac{x^2+2xh+h^2-2x-2h+10-x^2+2x-10}{h} = \lim\limits_{h \to 0} \frac{2xh+h^2-2h}{h} = \lim\limits_{h \to 0} \frac{h(2x+h-2)}{h}$$

$$= \lim_{h \to 0} \frac{\cancel{h}(2x+h-2)}{\cancel{h}} = \lim_{h \to 0} (2x+h-2) = 2x+0-2 = 2x-2$$

The instantaneous rate of change at $x = 1$ is $2(1) - 2 = 0$.

The instantaneous rate of change at $x = -5$ is $2(-5) - 2 = -10 - 2 = -12$.

9. Instantaneous rate of change in $f(x)$ at any $x = \lim_{h \to 0} \dfrac{f(x+h)-f(x)}{h}$.

$$\lim_{h \to 0} \frac{f(x+h)-f(x)}{h} = \lim_{h \to 0} \frac{\left[2(x+h)^3 - 2(x+h)^2 + 3(x+h) - 1\right] - \left[2x^3 - 2x^2 + 3x - 1\right]}{h}$$

$$= \lim_{h \to 0} \frac{2\left(x^3 + 3x^2h + 3xh^2 + h^3\right) - 2\left(x^2 + 2xh + h^2\right) + 3(x+h) - 1 - \left(2x^3 - 2x^2 + 3x - 1\right)}{h}$$

$$= \lim_{h \to 0} \frac{2x^3 + 6x^2h + 6xh^2 + 2h^3 - 2x^2 - 4xh - 2h^2 + 3x + 3h - 1 - 2x^3 + 2x^2 - 3x + 1}{h}$$

$$= \lim_{h \to 0} \frac{6x^2h + 6xh^2 + 2h^3 - 4xh - 2h^2 + 3h}{h} = \lim_{h \to 0} \frac{\cancel{h}\left(6x^2 + 6xh + 2h^2 - 4x - 2h + 3\right)}{\cancel{h}}, \; h \neq 0$$

$$= \lim_{h \to 0} \left(6x^2 + 6xh + 2h^2 - 4x - 2h + 3\right) = 6x^2 + 6x(0) + 2(0)^2 - 4x - 2(0) + 3 = 6x^2 - 4x + 3$$

The instantaneous rate of change at $x = 1$ is $6(1)^2 - 4(1) + 3 = 6 - 4 + 3 = 5$.

The instantaneous rate of change at $x = -5$ is $6(-5)^2 - 4(-5) + 3 = 150 + 20 + 3 = 173$.

11. Instantaneous rate of change in $f(x)$ at any $x = \lim_{h \to 0} \dfrac{f(x+h)-f(x)}{h}$

$$= \lim_{h \to 0} \frac{f(x+h)-f(x)}{h} = \lim_{h \to 0} \frac{\dfrac{x+h}{x+h+2} - \dfrac{x}{x+2}}{h} = \lim_{h \to 0} \frac{\dfrac{x+h}{x+h+2} \cdot \dfrac{(x+2)}{(x+2)} - \dfrac{x}{x+2} \cdot \dfrac{(x+h+2)}{(x+h+2)}}{h}$$

$$= \lim_{h \to 0} \frac{\dfrac{(x+h)(x+2) - x(x+h+2)}{(x+2)(x+h+2)}}{h} = \lim_{h \to 0} \frac{\dfrac{x^2 + 2x + hx + 2h - x^2 - xh - 2x}{(x+2)(x+h+2)}}{h}$$

$$= \lim_{h \to 0} \frac{\dfrac{2h}{(x+2)(x+h+2)}}{h} = \lim_{h \to 0} \left[\frac{2h}{(x+2)(x+h+2)} \div \frac{h}{1}\right] = \lim_{h \to 0} \left[\frac{2h}{(x+2)(x+h+2)} \cdot \frac{1}{h}\right]$$

$$= \lim_{h \to 0} \frac{2}{(x+2)(x+h+2)} = \frac{2}{(x+2)(x+0+2)} = \frac{2}{(x+2)(x+2)} = \frac{2}{(x+2)^2}$$

The instantaneous rate of change at $x = 1$ is $\frac{2}{(1+2)^2} = \frac{2}{3^2} = \frac{2}{9}$.

The instantaneous rate of change at $x = -5$ is $\frac{2}{(-5+2)^2} = \frac{2}{(-3)^2} = \frac{2}{9}$.

13. Instantaneous rate of change in $f(x)$ at any $x = \lim_{h \to 0} \frac{f(x+h) - f(x)}{h}$.

$$= \lim_{h \to 0} \frac{\frac{1}{(x+h)^2} - \frac{1}{x^2}}{h} = \lim_{h \to 0} \frac{\frac{1}{(x+h)^2} \cdot \frac{x^2}{x^2} - \frac{1}{x^2} \cdot \frac{(x+h)^2}{(x+h)^2}}{h} = \lim_{h \to 0} \frac{\frac{x^2}{x^2(x+h)^2} - \frac{(x+h)^2}{x^2(x+h)^2}}{h}$$

$$= \lim_{h \to 0} \frac{\frac{x^2 - (x+h)^2}{x^2(x+h)^2}}{h} = \lim_{h \to 0} \frac{\frac{x^2 - (x^2 + 2xh + h^2)}{x^2(x+h)^2}}{h} = \lim_{h \to 0} \frac{\frac{x^2 - x^2 - 2xh - h^2}{x^2(x+h)^2}}{h} = \lim_{h \to 0} \frac{\frac{-2xh - h^2}{x^2(x+h)^2}}{h}$$

$$= \lim_{h \to 0} \left[\frac{h(-2x-h)}{x^2(x+h)^2} \div \frac{h}{1} \right] = \lim_{h \to 0} \left[\frac{h(-2x-h)}{x^2(x+h)^2} \cdot \frac{1}{h} \right] = \lim_{h \to 0} \frac{-2x-h}{x^2(x+h)^2} = \frac{-2x-0}{x^2(x+0)^2}$$

$$= \frac{-2x}{x^2 \cdot x^2} = \frac{-2x}{x^4} = \frac{-2}{x^3}$$

The instantaneous rate of change at $x = 1$ is $\frac{-2}{(1)^3} = \frac{-2}{1} = -2$.

The instantaneous rate of change at $x = -5$ is $\frac{-2}{(-5)^3} = \frac{-2}{-125} = \frac{2}{125}$.

15. The average rate of change over [3, 5] $= \frac{y_2 - y_1}{x_2 - x_1} = \frac{7-7}{5-3} = \frac{0}{2} = 0$

The average rate of change over [5, 7] $= \frac{y_2 - y_1}{x_2 - x_1} = \frac{12-7}{7-5} = \frac{5}{2}$

The average rate of change over [4, 5] $= \frac{y_2 - y_1}{x_2 - x_1} = \frac{7-7}{5-4} = \frac{0}{1} = 0$

The average rate of change over [5, 6] $= \frac{y_2 - y_1}{x_2 - x_1} = \frac{12-7}{6-5} = \frac{5}{1} = 5$

The average rate of change over [5, 5.3] $= \frac{y_2 - y_1}{x_2 - x_1} = \frac{12-7}{5.3-5} = \frac{5}{0.3} = 16.7$

The average rate of change over [5, 5.3] $= \frac{y_2 - y_1}{x_2 - x_1} = \frac{12-7}{5.3-5} = \frac{5}{0.3} = 16.7$

The average rate of change over [5, 5.7] $= \dfrac{y_2-y_1}{x_2-x_1} = \dfrac{12-7}{5.7-5} = \dfrac{5}{0.7} = 7.1$

The average rate of change over [5, 5.3] $= \dfrac{y_2-y_1}{x_2-x_1} = \dfrac{12-7}{5.3-5} = \dfrac{5}{0.3} = 16.7$

The average rate of change over [5, 5.9] $= \dfrac{y_2-y_1}{x_2-x_1} = \dfrac{12-7}{5.9-5} = \dfrac{5}{0.9} = 5.6$

The average rate of change over [5, 5.1] $= \dfrac{y_2-y_1}{x_2-x_1} = \dfrac{12-7}{5.1-5} = \dfrac{5}{0.1} = 50$

The average rate of change over [5, 5.95] $= \dfrac{y_2-y_1}{x_2-x_1} = \dfrac{12-7}{5.95-5} = \dfrac{5}{0.95} = 5.3$

The average rate of change over [5, 5.05] $= \dfrac{y_2-y_1}{x_2-x_1} = \dfrac{12-7}{5.05-5} = \dfrac{5}{0.05} = 100$

The average rate of change over [5, 5.99] $= \dfrac{y_2-y_1}{x_2-x_1} = \dfrac{12-7}{5.99-5} = \dfrac{5}{0.99} = 5.1$

The average rate of change over [5, 5.01] $= \dfrac{y_2-y_1}{x_2-x_1} = \dfrac{12-7}{5.01-5} = \dfrac{5}{0.01} = 500$

The instantaneous rate of change at $x = 5$ does not exist.

17. (a) Firm's average growth rate in sales on [0, 7] $= \dfrac{R(x_2)-R(x_1)}{x_2-x_1}$.

$R(x_1) = R(0) = 3(0) + \frac{1}{2}(0)^2 = 0 + \frac{1}{2}(0) = 0.$

$R(x_2) = R(7) = 3(7) + \frac{1}{2}(7)^2 = 21 + \frac{1}{2}(49) = 21 + 24.5 = 45.5$

$\dfrac{R(x_2)-R(x_1)}{x_2-x_1} = \dfrac{45.5-0}{7-0} = \$6.5$ million per year.

(b) Firm's instantaneous rate of growth $= \lim\limits_{h \to 0} \dfrac{R(x+h)-R(x)}{h}$

$= \lim\limits_{h \to 0} \left[\dfrac{3(x+h)+\frac{1}{2}(x+h)^2 -\left(3x+\frac{1}{2}x^2\right)}{h} \right] = \lim\limits_{h \to 0} \dfrac{3x+3h+\frac{1}{2}\left(x^2 +2xh+h^2\right)-3x-\frac{1}{2}x^2}{h}$

$= \lim\limits_{h \to 0} \dfrac{3x+3h+\frac{1}{2}x^2 +xh+\frac{1}{2}h^2 -3x-\frac{1}{2}x^2}{h} = \lim\limits_{h \to 0} \dfrac{3h+xh}{h} = \lim\limits_{h \to 0} \dfrac{\not{h}(3+x)}{\not{h}}$

$= \lim\limits_{h \to 0} (3+x) = 3+x$

Firm's instantaneous rate of growth after its seventh year $= 3 + 7 = \$10$ million per year.

(c) $R(10) = 3(10) + \frac{1}{2}(10)^2 = 30 + \frac{1}{2}(100) = 30 + 50 = \$80$ million per year.

(d) If the growth in sales after the seventh year always equals the growth achieved at the end of the seventh year, then the firm's total sales at the end of the tenth year

is $R(7) + 3(3 + 7) = \left[3(7) + \frac{1}{2}(7)^2\right] + 3(10) = 21 + \frac{1}{2}(49) + 30 = \$75.5$ million per year.

Section 4.5: The Derivative

1. $f'(x) = 5x^{5-1} - 7(3x^{3-1}) + 4 + 0 = 5x^4 - 21x^2 + 4$

3. $f'(x) = 7x^{7-1} + 6(3x^{3-1}) - 4(2x^{2-1}) = 7x^6 + 18x^2 - 8x$

5. First, rewrite $f(x)$ as $f(x) = \frac{1}{5}x^5 - \frac{1}{3}x^3 - \frac{1}{2}x^2 + 10$.

   Then, $f'(x) = \frac{1}{5}(5x^{5-1}) - \frac{1}{3}(3x^{3-1}) - \frac{1}{2}(2x^{2-1}) + 0 = \frac{5}{5}x^4 - \frac{3}{3}x^2 - \frac{2}{2}x = x^4 - x^2 - x$

7. First, expand the product by using the FOIL method.

   We have: $f(x) = x^2(x^5) + x^2(3) + 4(x^5) + 4(3) = x^7 + 3x^2 + 4x^5 + 12$

   Then, $f'(x) = 7x^{7-1} + 3(2x^{2-1}) + 4(5x^{5-1}) + 0 = 7x^6 + 6x + 20x^4 = 7x^6 + 20x^4 + 6x$

9. $f'(x) = 10 \cdot e^x = 10e^x$, since the derivative of e^x is e^x.

11. $f'(x) = 4x^{4-1} - 7(2x^{2-1}) + (7e)e^x = 4x^3 - 14x + 7e^x$

13. Using the distributive property, $f(x)$ becomes: $f(x) = x^3 + 2x^2 + 8e^x$.

   Then, $f'(x) = 3x^{3-1} + 2(2x^{2-1}) + 8e^x = 3x^2 + 4x + 8e^x$

15. First, simplify $f(x)$ by factoring the numerator. Then, cancel the factor $(x + 2)$. We have:

   $f(x) = \dfrac{(x+10)\cancel{(x+2)}}{\cancel{x+2}} = x + 10$, if $x \neq -2$. Therefore, $f'(x) = 1 + 0 = 1$.

17. $\dfrac{dy}{dx} = 7x^{7-1} + 6(5x^{5-1}) + 3 + 0 = 7x^6 + 30x^4 + 3$

19. Rewrite y to $y = x^5 - \frac{1}{4}x^4 + 7e^x$.

   Then, $\dfrac{dy}{dx} = 5x^{5-1} - \frac{1}{4}(4x^{4-1}) + 7e^x = 5x^4 - \frac{4}{4}x^3 + 7e^x = 5x^4 - x^3 + 7e^x$

21. Rewrite y to $y = \frac{1}{4}x^4 - \frac{1}{3}x^3 - \frac{1}{2}x^2$.

   Then, $\dfrac{dy}{dx} = \frac{1}{4}(4x^{4-1}) - \frac{1}{3}(3x^{3-1}) - \frac{1}{2}(2x^{2-1}) = \frac{4}{4}x^3 - \frac{3}{3}x^2 - \frac{2}{2}x = x^3 - x^2 - x$

23. Expand the product by using the FOIL method. We have:

$$y = x^2(x) - x^2(3) + 2(x) - 2(3) = x^3 - 3x^2 + 2x - 6.$$

Then, $\dfrac{dy}{dx} = 3x^{3-1} - 3(2x^{2-1}) + 2 - 0 = 3x^2 - 6x + 2$

25. (a) $S'(x) = 0 + 6,000 - 50(2x^{2-1}) = 6,000 - 100x$

(b) At $x = 45$, $S'(45) = 6,000 - 100(45) = \$6,000 - \$4,500 = \$1,500$. Yes. At an advertising expenditure of \$45,000, there is an increase in sales at \$1,500.

At $x = 60$, $S'(60) = 6000 - 100(60) = 6000 - 6000 = \$0$. This means, if the company spends more than \$60,000 in advertising, the amount of sales will actually decline.

27. (a) Average rate of change over [0, 4] $= \dfrac{D(t_2) - D(t_1)}{t_2 - t_1} = \dfrac{2 - 0}{4 - 0} = \dfrac{2}{4}$. This means, every 2 miles traveled, it will take 4 minutes. Using dimensional analysis, we have:

$$\frac{2\ mi}{4\ min} = \frac{2\ mi}{4\ min} \cdot \frac{60\ min}{1\ hr} = \frac{120\ mi}{4\ hr} = 30 \text{ mph}$$

(b)

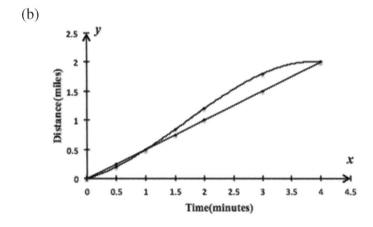

(c) $D'(t) = -0.05(3t^{3-1}) + 0.25(2t^{2-1}) + 0.3 = -0.15t^2 + 0.5t + 0.3.$

$D'(1) = -0.15(1)^2 + 0.5(1) + 0.3 = -0.15 + 0.5 + 0.3 = 0.65$

The speed of Mr. Williams' car at exactly 1 minute after the start of his trip is 0.65 mile per minute. Using dimensional analysis, we have:

$$D'(1) = \frac{0.65\ mi}{1\ min} = \frac{0.65 mi}{1 min} \cdot \frac{60 min}{1\ hr} = \frac{39 mi}{1 hr} = 39 \text{ mph}.$$

(d) We need to find the equation of a tangent line to the curve
$D(t) = -0.05t^3 + 0.25t^2 + 0.3t$ at $(1, D(1)) = (1, 0.5)$. Since $m = D'(1) = 0.65$, $y = 0.65t + b$. Use the point $(1, 0.5)$ to find b. We have:

$$0.5 = 0.65(1) + b$$
$$0.5 = 0.65 + b$$
$$-0.65 \quad -0.65$$
$$b = -0.15$$

Therefore, the equation of a tangent line to the curve $D(t) = -0.05t^3 + 0.25t^2 + 0.3t$ at $(1, 0.5)$ is $y = 0.65t - 0.15$.

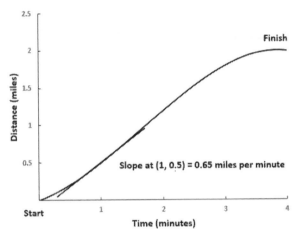

(e) $D'(4) = -0.15(4)^2 + 0.5(4) + 0.3 = -2.4 + 2 + 0.3 = -0.1$ mile per minute. Using dimensional analysis, we have:

$$D'(4) = \frac{-0.1 \ mi}{1 \ min} \cdot \frac{60 \ min}{1 \ hr} = \frac{-6 \ mi}{1 \ hr} = -6 \text{ miles per hour}$$

29. (a) $D'(p) = 30(2p^{2-1}) + 5 + 0 = 60p + 5 > 0, for \ p > 0.$ That is, as p increases positively, $D(p)$ increases. Therefore, no.

(b) Rewrite $D(p) = 3000p^{-1}$.

   Then, $D'(p) = 3000(-1p^{-1-1}) = -3000p^{-2} = \frac{-3000}{p^2}$. We see that $D'(p) < 0$ for $p > 0$. This means, when p increases positively, $D(p)$ decreases. Therefore, yes.

(c) $D'(p) = 5(2p^{2-1}) - 0 = 10p > 0$ for $p > 0$. This means, as p increases positively, $D(p)$ increases (is positive). Therefore, no.

(d) $D'(p) = 5(2p^{2-1}) - 2000 = 10p - 2000.$ For $0 \le p < 200, D(p) < 0$(decreases). For $p > 200, \ D(p) > 0.$This means, as p increases over 200, $D(p)$ increases (is positive). Therefore, no.

Section 4.6: Additional Rules

1. There are two ways to compute $f'(x)$ for $f(x) = (x^2 + 3x)(x^5 + x^7 + 2x)$.

   <u>**Method 1**</u>: Expand the product. We have:

   $$f(x) = x^2(x^5 + x^7 + 2x) + 3x(x^5 + x^7 + 2x)$$
   $$= x^2(x^5) + x^2(x^7) + x^2(2x) + 3x(x^5) + 3x(x^7) + 3x(2x)$$
   $$= x^{2+5} + x^{2+7} + 2x^{2+1} + 3x^{1+5} + 3x^{1+7} + 6x^{1+1}$$
   $$= x^7 + x^9 + 2x^3 + 3x^6 + 3x^8 + 6x^2$$

   Then, $f'(x) = 7(x^{7-1}) + 9x^{9-1} + 2(3x^{3-1}) + 3(6x^{6-1}) + 3(8x^{8-1}) + 6(2x^{2-1})$
   $$= 7x^6 + 9x^8 + 6x^2 + 18x^5 + 24x^7 + 12x$$
   $$= 9x^8 + 24x^7 + 7x^6 + 18x^5 + 6x^2 + 12x$$

   <u>**Method 2**</u>: Use the Product Rule with $g(x) = x^2 + 3x$ and $h(x) = x^5 + x^7 + 2x$.

   $$f'(x) = h(x) \cdot g'(x) + g(x) \cdot h'(x)$$
   $$= (x^5 + x^7 + 2x)(2x^{2-1} + 3) + (x^2 + 3x)(5x^{5-1} + 7x^{7-1} + 2)$$
   $$= (x^5 + x^7 + 2x)(2x + 3) + (x^2 + 3x)(5x^4 + 7x^6 + 2)$$
   $$= x^5(2x + 3) + x^7(2x + 3) + 2x(2x + 3) + x^2(5x^4 + 7x^6 + 2) + 3x(5x^4 + 7x^6 + 2)$$
   $$= 2x^6 + 3x^5 + 2x^8 + 3x^7 + 4x^2 + 6x + 5x^6 + 7x^8 + 2x^2 + 15x^5 + 21x^7 + 6x$$
   $$= 9x^8 + 24x^7 + 7x^6 + 18x^5 + 6x^2 + 12x$$

3. $f'(x) = -5x^{-5-1} + (-3)x^{-3-1} + (-2)x^{-2-1} = -5x^{-6} - 3x^{-4} - 2x^{-3}$
   $$= -\frac{5}{x^6} - \frac{3}{x^4} - \frac{2}{x^3}$$

5. $f'(x) = -\frac{5}{2}x^{-\frac{5}{2}-1} + \left(-\frac{1}{2}\right)x^{-\frac{1}{2}-1} = -\frac{5}{2}x^{-7/2} - \frac{1}{2}x^{-3/2} = -\frac{5}{2x^{7/2}} - \frac{1}{2x^{3/2}}$

7. **(Quotient Rule)**

   The derivative of the function $f(x) = \dfrac{N(x)}{D(x)}$ is $f'(x) = \dfrac{D(x) \cdot N'(x) - N(x) \cdot D'(x)}{[D(x)]^2}$,

   with $N(x) = x^3 + x^5$ and $D(x) = x^2 + x^4$. We have:

   $$f'(x) = \frac{(x^2 + x^4)(3x^{3-1} + 5x^{5-1}) - (x^3 + x^5)(2x^{2-1} + 4x^{4-1})}{(x^2 + x^4)^2}$$

$$= \frac{(x^2+x^4)(3x^2+5x^4)-(x^3+x^5)(2x+4x^3)}{(x^2+x^4)^2}$$

$$= \frac{x^2(3x^2+5x^4)+x^4(3x^2+5x^4)-x^3(2x+4x^3)-x^5(2x+4x^3)}{(x^2+x^4)^2}$$

$$= \frac{x^2(3x^2)+x^2(5x^4)+x^4(3x^2)+x^4(5x^4)-x^3(2x)-x^3(4x^3)-x^5(2x)-x^5(4x^3)}{(x^2+x^4)^2}$$

$$= \frac{3x^4+5x^6+3x^6+5x^8-2x^4-4x^6-2x^6-4x^8}{(x^2+x^4)^2}$$

$$= \frac{x^8+2x^6+x^4}{(x^2+x^4)^2}$$

9. **(Quotient Rule)**

The derivative of the function $f(x) = \frac{N(x)}{D(x)}$ is $f'(x) = \frac{D(x)\cdot N'(x)-N(x)\cdot D'(x)}{[D(x)]^2}$,

with $N(x) = e^{4x}$ and $D(x) = x^5 - x^{-3}$. We have:

$$f'(x) = \frac{(x^5-x^{-3})(4e^{4x})-(e^{4x})(5x^{5-1}-(-3)x^{-3-1})}{(x^5-x^{-3})^2}$$

$$= \frac{(x^5-x^{-3})(4e^{4x})-(e^{4x})(5x^4+3x^{-4})}{(x^5-x^{-3})^2}$$

$$= \frac{x^5(4e^{4x})-x^{-3}(4e^{4x})-e^{4x}(5x^4)-e^{4x}(3x^{-4})}{(x^5-x^{-3})^2}$$

$$= \frac{4x^5e^{4x}-4x^{-3}e^{4x}-5x^4e^{4x}-3x^{-4}e^{4x}}{(x^5-x^{-3})^2}$$

11. **(Product Rule)**

The derivative of $f(x) = g(x) \cdot h(x)$ is $f'(x) = h(x) \cdot g'(x) + g(x) \cdot h'(x)$, with $g(x) = e^{7x}$ and $h(x) = x^7$. We have:

$$f'(x) = x^7(7e^{7x}) + e^{7x}(7x^{7-1}) = 7x^7e^{7x} + 7x^6e^{7x} = 7x^6e^{7x}(x + 1)$$

13. The derivative of the function $f(x) = \frac{N(x)}{D(x)}$ is $f'(x) = \frac{D(x)\cdot N'(x)-N(x)\cdot D'(x)}{[D(x)]^2}$,

with $g(x) = x^6 + 7$ and $h(x) = x^5 + 3x$. We have:

$$f'(x) = \frac{(x^5 + 3x)(6x^{6-1} + 0) - (x^6 + 7)(5x^{5-1} + 3)}{(x^5 + 3x)^2}$$

$$= \frac{(x^5 + 3x)(6x^5) - (x^6 + 7)(5x^4 + 3)}{(x^5 + 3x)^2}$$

$$= \frac{x^5(6x^5) + 3x(6x^5) - x^6(5x^4 + 3) - 7(5x^4 + 3)}{(x^5 + 3x)^2}$$

$$= \frac{6x^{10} + 18x^6 - x^6(5x^4) - x^6(3) - 7(5x^4) - 7(3)}{(x^5 + 3x)^2}$$

$$= \frac{6x^{10} + 18x^6 - 5x^{10} - 3x^6 - 35x^4 - 21}{(x^5 + 3x)^2} = \frac{x^{10} + 15x^6 - 35x^4 - 21}{(x^5 + 3x)^2}$$

$$= \frac{x^{10} + 15x^6 - 35x^4 - 21}{x^{10} + 6x^6 + 9x^2}$$

15. $f'(x) = 5(x^7 + 6x)^{5-1} \cdot \frac{d}{dx}(x^7 + 6x)$

$= 5(x^7 + 6x)^4(7x^{7-1} + 6) = 5(x^7 + 6x)^4(7x^6 + 6)$

17. $f'(x) = 3(x^4 + 3x^2 + 4x + 2)^{3-1} \frac{d}{dx}(x^4 + 3x^2 + 4x + 2)$

$= 3(x^4 + 3x^2 + 4x + 2)^2(4x^{4-1} + 3(2x^{2-1}) + 4 + 0)$

$= 3(x^4 + 3x^2 + 4x + 2)^2(4x^3 + 6x + 4)$

19. (**Product Rule**)

The derivative of $y = g(x) \cdot h(x)$ is $\frac{dy}{dx} = h(x) \cdot g'(x) + g(x) \cdot h'(x)$, with $g(x) = e^{10x}$ and $h(x) = x^3$.

$\frac{dy}{dx} = x^3(10e^{10x}) + e^{10x}(3x^{3-1}) = 10x^3 e^{10x} + 3x^2 e^{10x} = x^2 e^{10x}(10x + 3)$

21. $\frac{dy}{dx} = 5x^{5-1} + 3(-5x^{-5-1}) = 5x^4 - 15x^{-6} = 5x^4 - \frac{15}{x^6}$

23. First, rewrite y as $y = x^{-5} + x^{-4}$. Then,

$\frac{dy}{dx} = -5x^{-5-1} + (-4x^{-4-1}) = -5x^{-6} - 4x^{-5} = \frac{-5}{x^6} - \frac{4}{x^5}$

25. $\frac{dy}{dx} = \frac{3}{2}x^{\frac{3}{2}-1} + 7\left(\frac{5}{2}x^{\frac{5}{2}-1}\right) = \frac{3}{2}x^{1/2} + \left(7 \cdot \frac{5}{2}\right)x^{3/2} = \frac{3}{2}x^{1/2} + \frac{35}{2}x^{3/2}$

27. $\frac{dS}{dx} = \frac{dS}{dE} \cdot \frac{dE}{dx} = (2E^{2-1} + 3)(2x^{2-1}) = (2E + 3)(2x) = (2x^2 + 3)(2x)$

$\quad = 4x^3 + 6x$

29. $\frac{dS}{dx} = \frac{dS}{dE} \cdot \frac{dE}{dx} = \left[\frac{(E+2)(1) - E(1)}{(E+2)^2}\right] \cdot (3 \cdot 2x^{2-1}) = \left[\frac{E+2-E}{(E+2)^2}\right] \cdot (3 \cdot 2x^{2-1}) = \left[\frac{2}{(E+2)^2}\right] \cdot 6x$

$\quad = \frac{2}{(E+2)^2} \cdot \frac{6x}{1} = \frac{12x}{(E+2)^2} = \frac{12x}{(3x^2+5+2)^2} = \frac{12x}{(3x^2+7)^2} = \frac{12x}{9x^4+42x^2+49}$

Section 4.7: Higher Order Derivatives

1. **Part 1**

$\frac{dy}{dx} = 5x^{5-1} + 4(2x^{2-1}) + 3 = 5x^4 + 8x + 3$

$\frac{d^2y}{dx^2} = \frac{d}{dx}\left(5x^4 + 8x + 3\right) = 5\left(4x^{4-1}\right) + 8 + 0 = 20x^3 + 8$

Part 2

For $x = 1$, $\frac{d^2y}{dx^2} = 20(1)^3 + 8 = 20 + 8 = 28$.

For $x = 2$, $\frac{d^2y}{dx^2} = 20(2)^3 + 8 = 20 \cdot 8 + 8 = 160 + 8 = 168$.

3. **Part 1**

$\frac{dy}{dx} = 4x^{4-1} + 3(2x^{2-1}) + 4 + 0 = 4x^3 + 6x + 4$

$\frac{d^2y}{dx^2} = \frac{d}{dx}\left(4x^3 + 6x + 4\right) = 4\left(3x^{3-1}\right) + 6 + 0 = 12x^2 + 6$

Part 2

For $x = 1$, $\frac{d^2y}{dx^2} = 12(1)^2 + 6 = 12 + 6 = 18$

For $x = 2$, $\frac{d^2y}{dx^2} = 12(2)^2 + 6 = 12(4) + 6 = 48 + 6 = 54$

5. **Part 1** (**Product Rule**)

The derivative of $y = g(x) \cdot h(x)$ is $\frac{dy}{dx} = h(x) \cdot g'(x) + g(x) \cdot h'(x)$, with $g(x) = x^3$ and $h(x) = e^{10x}$.

$$\frac{dy}{dx} = e^{10x}(3x^{3-1}) + x^3(10e^{10x}) = 3x^2 e^{10x} + 10x^3 e^{10x} = (3x^2 + 10x^3)e^{10x}$$

Apply the Product Rule again for each term in $\frac{dy}{dx}$.

$$\frac{d^2y}{dx^2} = \frac{d}{dx}(3x^2 + 10x^3)e^{10x}$$

$$= (3x^2 + 10x^3)(10e^{10x}) + e^{10x}(3 \cdot 2x^{2-1} + 10 \cdot 3x^{3-1})$$

$$= 10(3x^2 + 10x^3)e^{10x} + e^{10x}(6x + 30x^2)$$

$$= 30x^2 e^{10x} + 100x^3 e^{10x} + 6x e^{10x} + 30x^2 e^{10x} = 6x e^{10x} + 60x^2 e^{10x} + 100x^3 e^{10x}$$

$$= (6x + 60x^2 + 100x^3)e^{10x}$$

Part 2

For $x = 1$, $\frac{d^2y}{dx^2} = [6(1) + 60(1)^2 + 100(1)^3]e^{10(1)} = (6 + 60 + 100)e^{10} = 166e^{10}$

For $x = 2$, $\frac{d^2y}{dx^2} = [6(2) + 60(2)^2 + 100(2)^3]e^{10(1)} = (12 + 240 + 800)e^{20} = 1052e^{20}$

7. (a) $speed = D'(t) = -0.05(3t^{3-1}) + 0.25(2t^{2-1}) + 0.3 = -0.15t^2 + 0.5t + 0.3$

   (b) $D'(1) = -0.15(1)^2 + 0.5(1) + 0.3 = -0.15 + 0.5 + 0.3 = 0.65.$ The speed of Mr. Williams' car at exactly 1 minute after the start of his trip is 0.65 mile per minute. Using dimensional analysis, we have:

   $$D'(1) = \frac{0.65\ mi}{1\ min} = \frac{0.65mi}{1min} \cdot \frac{60min}{1\ hr} = \frac{39mi}{1hr} = 39 \text{ mph.}$$

   (c) $Acceleration = D''(t) = \frac{d^2D}{dt^2} = \frac{d}{dx}(-0.15t^2 + 0.5t + 0.3) = -0.15(2t^{2-1}) + 0.5$

   $$= -0.3t + 0.5$$

   (d) At $t = 1$, $D''(1) = -0.3(1) + 0.5 = -0.3 + 0.5 = 0.2$ mile per minute^2. Using dimensional analysis, we have:

   $$D''(1) = \frac{0.2\ mi}{1\ min} = \frac{0.2\ mi}{1min^2} \cdot \frac{60min}{1\ hr} \cdot \frac{60min}{1\ hr} = \frac{mi}{hr^2} = 720 \text{ mph}^2.$$

   At $t = 3$, $D''(3) = -0.3(3) + 0.5 = -0.9 + 0.5 = -0.4$ mile per minute^2. Using dimensional analysis, we have:

$$D''(3) = \frac{-0.4\ mi}{1\ min} = \frac{-0.4\ mi}{1min} \cdot \frac{60min}{1\ hr} \cdot \frac{60min}{1\ hr} = \frac{-1440\ mi}{hr^2} = -1440 \text{ mph}^2.$$ This means,

Mr. William had decreased his speed(decelerated) by 1440 mph^2 in 3 minutes.

Chapter 5 Applications of the Derivative

Section 5.1: Optimization through Differentiation

1.

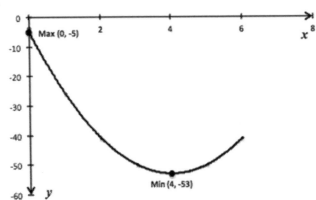

Differentiating the given function, we have: $\dfrac{dy}{dx} = 3(2x^{2-1}) - 24 - 0 = 6x - 24$. To locate all values of x for which the derivative is 0, we set the derivative function to zero and solve for x.

$$6x - 24 = 0$$
$$+24\ \ +24$$
$$6x = 24$$
$$\frac{6x}{6} = \frac{24}{6}$$
$$x = 4$$

The derivative exists everywhere, and the endpoints are $x = 0$ and $x = 6$. Evaluating the function at $x = 0$, $x = 4$, and $x = 6$, we have:

$$x = 0,\ y = 3(0)^2 - 24(0) - 5 = 0 - 0 - 5 = -5$$

$$x = 4,\ y = 3(4)^2 - 24(4) - 5 = 48 - 96 - 5 = -53$$

$$x = 6,\ y = 3(6)^2 - 24(6) - 5 = 108 - 144 - 5 = -41$$

It follows that the maximum is $y = -5$ occurring at $x = 0$, and the minimum is $y = -53$ occurring at $x = 4$.

3.

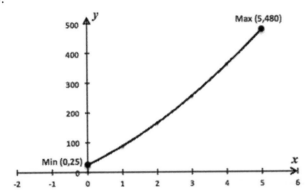

Differentiating the given function, we have: $\frac{dy}{dx} = 7(2x^{2-1}) + 56 + 0 = 14x + 56$. To locate all values of x for which the derivative is 0, we set the derivative to zero and solve for x.

$14x + 56 = 0$

$\quad -56 \quad -56$

$14x = -56$

$\frac{14x}{14} = \frac{-56}{14}$

$x = -4$

Because $x = -4$ is outside our domain and is not an allowable point for this problem, we disregard it. The derivative exists everywhere, and the endpoints are $x = 0$ and $x = 5$. Evaluating the function at $x = 0$ and $x = 5$, we have:

$x = 0, y = 7(0)^2 + 56(0) + 25 = 25$

$x = 5, y = 7(5)^2 + 56(5) + 25 = 175 + 280 + 25 = 480$

It follows that the maximum is $y = 480$ occurring at $x = 5$, and the minimum is $y = 25$ occurring at $x = 0$.

5.

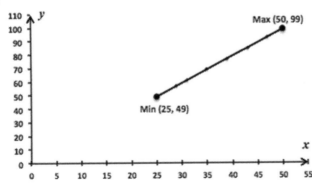

Differentiating the given function, we have $\frac{dy}{dx} = 2 > 0$. The derivative is 2 everywhere and never equals 0. Therefore, maximum and minimum will occur at the endpoints $x = 25$ and $x = 50$. Evaluating the function at $x = 25$ and $x = 50$, we have:

$x = 25, y = 2(25) - 1 = 50 - 1 = 49$

$x = 50, y = 2(50) - 1 = 100 - 1 = 99$

It follows that the maximum is $y = 99$ occurring at $x = 50$, and the minimum is $y = 49$ occurring at $x = 25$.

7. Differentiating the given function, we have: $D'(t) = 3t^{3-1} - 12 + 0 = 3t^2 - 12$. To locate all values of t for which the derivative is 0, we set the derivative to zero and solve for t.

$3t^2 - 12 = 0$

$3(t^2 - 4) = 0$

$3(t + 2)(t - 2) = 0$

$t + 2 = 0$ or $t - 2 = 0$

$t = -2$ or $t = 2$

$t = -2$ and $t = 2$ are both in the interval $-4 \leq t \leq 4$. Therefore, the values will be included in calculating possible maximum and minimum values.

The derivative exists everywhere, and the endpoints are $t = -4$ and $t = 4$. Evaluating the function at $t = -4$, $t = -2, t = 2$, and $t = 4$, we have:

$t = -4, D = (-4)^3 - 12(-4) + 7 = -64 + 48 + 7 = -9$

$t = -2, D = (-2)^3 - 12(-2) + 7 = -8 + 24 + 7 = 23$

$t = 2, D = (2)^3 - 12(2) + 7 = 8 - 24 + 7 = -9$

$t = 4, D = (4)^3 - 12(4) + 7 = 64 - 48 + 7 = 23$

It follows that the maximum is $D = 23$ occurring at $t = -2$ and $t = 4$, and the minimum is $D = -9$ occurring at $t = -4$ and $t = 2$.

9. Differentiating the given function, we have $D'(t) = 3t^{3-1} - 12 + 0 = 3t^2 - 12$. To locate all values of t for which the derivative is 0, we set the derivative to zero and solve for t.

$3t^2 - 12 = 0$

$3(t^2 - 4) = 0$

$3(t + 2)(t - 2) = 0$

$t + 2 = 0$ or $t - 2 = 0$

$t = -2$ or $t = 2$

Because $t = -2$ is outside our domain and is not an allowable point for this problem, we disregard it. The derivative exists everywhere, and the endpoints are $t = 0$ and $t = 3$. Evaluating the function at $t = 0$, $t = 2$, and $t = 3$, we have:

$t = 0, D = (0)^3 - 12(0) + 7 = 0 - 0 + 7 = 7$

$t = 2, D = (2)^3 - 12(2) + 7 = 8 - 24 + 7 = -9$

$t = 3, D = (3)^3 - 12(3) + 7 = 27 - 36 + 7 = -2$

It follows that the maximum is $D = 7$ occurring at $t = 0$, and the minimum is $D = -9$ occurring at $t = 2$.

11. Differentiating the given function, we have:

$y'(t) = 3t^{3-1} + 3(2t^{2-1}) - 105 + 0 = 3t^2 + 6t - 105$

To locate all values of t for which the derivative is 0, we set the derivative to zero and solve for t.

$3t^2 + 6t - 105 = 0$ $t + 7 = 0$ or $t - 5 = 0$

$3(t^2 + 2t - 35) = 0$ $t = -7$ $t = 5$

$3(t + 7)(t - 5) = 0$

$t = -7$ and $t = 5$ are both in the interval $-10 \le t \le 10$. Therefore, the values will be included in calculating possible maximum and minimum values.

The derivative exists everywhere, and the endpoints are $t = -10$ and $t = 10$. Evaluating the function at $t = -10$, $t = -7$, $t = 5$, and $t = 10$, we have:

$t = -10, \ y(-10) = (-10)^3 + 3(-10)^2 - 105(-10) + 20 = 370$

$t = -7, \ y(-7) = (-7)^3 + 3(-7)^2 - 105(-7) + 20 = 559$

$t = 5, \ y(5) = (5)^3 + 3(5)^2 - 105(5) + 20 = -305$

$t = 10, \ y(10) = (10)^3 + 3(10)^2 - 105(10) + 20 = 270$

It follows that the maximum is $y = 559$ occurring at $t = -7$, and the minimum is $y = -305$ occurring at $t = 5$.

13. Differentiating the given function, we have:

$x'(t) = \frac{1}{3}(3t^{3-1}) - 4(2t^{2-1}) + 0 = \frac{3}{3}t^2 - 8t = t^2 - 8t$. To locate all values of t for which the derivative is 0, we set the derivative to zero and solve for t.

$$t^2 - 8t = 0$$

$$t(t - 8) = 0$$

$$t = 0 \ \text{ or } \ t - 8 = 0$$

$$t = 0 \ \ or \ \ t = 8$$

The derivative exists everywhere, and the endpoints are $t = 0$ and $t = 9$. Evaluating the function at $t = 0$, $t = 8$, and $t = 9$, we have:

$$t = 0, x = \frac{1}{3}(0)^3 - 4(0)^2 + 12 = 0 - 0 + 12 = 12$$

$$t = 8, x = \frac{1}{3}(8)^3 - 4(8)^2 + 12 = \frac{512}{3} - 256 + 12 = \frac{512}{3} - 244 = \frac{512}{3} - \frac{732}{3} = -\frac{220}{3}$$

$$t = 9, x = \frac{1}{3}(9)^3 - 4(9)^2 + 12 = \frac{729}{3} - 324 + 12 = \frac{729}{3} - 312 = \frac{729}{3} - \frac{936}{3} = -\frac{207}{3} = -67$$

It follows that the maximum is $x = 12$ occurring at $t = 0$, and the minimum is $x = -\frac{220}{3}$ occurring at $t = 8$.

15. This problem can be solved by two methods.

Method 1: Expanding the Product

Expanding the product, we have $y(x) = x^2 - 20x - 10x + 200 = x^2 - 30x + 200$. Differentiating the given function, we have $y'(x) = 2x^{2-1} - 30 + 0 = 2x - 30$. To locate all values of x for which the derivative is 0, we set the derivative to zero and solve for x.

$$2x - 30 = 0$$

$$2x = 30$$

$$\frac{2x}{2} = \frac{30}{2}$$

$$x = 15$$

Method 2: Using the Product Rule

The derivative of $y = g(x) \cdot h(x)$ with $g(x) = x - 10$ and $h(x) = x - 20$ is:

$$f'(x) = h(x) \cdot g'(x) + g(x) \cdot h'(x)$$
$$= (x - 20)(1) + (x - 10)(1) = x - 20 + x - 10 = 2x - 30.$$

To locate all values of x for which the derivative is 0, we set the derivative to zero and solve for x. We have:

$$2x - 30 = 0 \qquad\qquad\qquad \frac{2x}{2} = \frac{30}{2}$$
$$+30 \quad +30 \qquad\qquad\qquad x = 15$$
$$2x = 30$$

The derivative exists everywhere, and the endpoints are $x = 5$ and $x = 25$. Evaluating the function at $x = 5$, $x = 15$, and $x = 25$, we have:

$x = 5$, $y = (5 - 10)(5 - 20) = (-5)(-15) = 75$

$x = 15$, $y = (15 - 10)(15 - 20) = (5)(-5) = -25$

$x = 25$, $y = (25 - 10)(25 - 20) = (15)(5) = 75$

It follows that the maximum is $y = 75$ occurring at $x = 5$ and $x = 25$, and the minimum is $y = -25$ occurring at $x = 15$.

17. (a) Rewrite the given function as $P = 22x - \frac{1}{2,000}x^2 - 10,000$. Differentiating the given function, we have:

$$P'(x) = 22 - \frac{1}{2,000}(2x^{2-1}) - 0 = 22 - \frac{2}{2,000}x = 22 - \frac{1}{1,000}x.$$

To locate all values of x for which the derivative is 0, we set the derivative to zero and solve for x.

$$22 - \frac{1}{1,000}x = 0$$

$$22 = \frac{1}{1,000}x$$

$$22 \cdot 1,000 = 1,000 \cdot \frac{1}{1,000}x$$

$$22,000 = \frac{1,000x}{1,000}$$

$$x = 22,000 \text{ items}$$

(b) If the manufacturer produced 22,000 items, its maximum profit is

$$P(22,000) = 22(22,000) - \frac{(22,000)^2}{2,000} - 10,000 = 484,000 - 242,000 - 10,000$$
$$= \$232,000$$

19. (a) Profit = Revenue – Total Cost

$$P(x) = 300x - (2.5x^2 - 200x + 20,000) = 300x - 2.5x^2 + 200x - 20,000$$
$$= -2.5x^2 + 500x - 20,000.$$

Differentiating the given function, we have:

$$P'(x) = -2.5(2x^{2-1}) + 500 - 0 = -5x + 500.$$

To locate all values of x for which the derivative is 0, we set the derivative to zero and solve for x.

$$-5x + 500 = 0$$

$$-5x = -500$$

$$\frac{-5x}{-5} = \frac{-500}{-5}$$

$$x = 100 \text{ refrigerators}$$

(b) If the manufacturer produces 100 refrigerators, the profit is:

$$P(100) = -2.5(100)^2 + 500(100) - 20{,}000$$

$$= -25{,}000 + 50{,}000 - 20{,}000 = \$5{,}000$$

(c) $C(100) = 2.5(100)^2 - 200(100) + 20{,}000 = 25{,}000 - 20{,}000 + 20{,}000 = \$25{,}000$

21. Profit = Revenue – Total Cost

$$P(x) = 325x - \left(\tfrac{1}{3}x^3 - 10x^2 - 800x + 12{,}000\right)$$

$$= 325x - \tfrac{1}{3}x^3 + 10x^2 + 800x - 12{,}000$$

$$= -\tfrac{1}{3}x^3 + 10x^2 + 1{,}125x - 12{,}000.$$

Differentiating the given function, we have:

$$P'(x) = -\tfrac{1}{3}(3x^{3-1}) + 10(2x^{2-1}) + 1{,}125 - 0 = -\tfrac{3}{3}x^2 + 20x + 1{,}125$$

$$= -x^2 + 20x + 1{,}125$$

To locate all values of x for which the derivative is 0, we set the derivative to zero and solve for x.

$$-x^2 + 20x + 1{,}125 = 0$$

Use the quadratic formula, with $a = -1, b = 20,$ and $c = 1{,}125,$ to solve for x.

$$x = \frac{-b \pm \sqrt{b^2 - 4ac}}{2a} = \frac{-20 \pm \sqrt{(20)^2 - 4(-1)(1{,}125)}}{2(-1)} = \frac{-20 \pm \sqrt{400 + 4{,}500}}{-2}$$

$$= \frac{-20 \pm \sqrt{4{,}900}}{-2} = \frac{-20 \pm 70}{-2}$$

$$x_1 = \frac{-20 + 70}{-2} = \frac{50}{-2} = -25 \quad \text{or} \quad x_2 = \frac{-20 - 70}{-2} = \frac{-90}{-2} = 45$$

Since x represents the number of units produced/sold, it cannot be negative. Therefore, the only solution is 45 units.

23. For $0 \le x \le 2$, differentiate the function $y(x) = -x^2 + 2x + 5$. We have $y'(x) = -2x^{2-1} + 2 + 0 = -2x + 2$. To locate all values of x for which the derivative is 0, we set the derivative to zero and solve for x.

$$-2x + 2 = 0$$

$$-2x = -2$$

$$\frac{-2x}{-2} = \frac{-2}{-2}$$

$$x = 1$$

For $2 < x \le 5$, differentiate the function $y(x) = x^2 - 8x + 16$. We have
$y'(x) = 2x^{2-1} - 8 + 0 = 2x - 8$. To locate all values of x for which the derivative is 0, we set the derivative to zero and solve for x.

$2x - 8 = 0$

$2x = 8$

$\dfrac{2x}{2} = \dfrac{8}{2}$

$x = 4$

Evaluating the function at $x = 0$, $x = 1$, $x = 2$, $x = 4$, and $x = 5$ we have:

$x = 0, y = -(0)^2 + 2(0) + 5 = 0 + 0 + 5 = 5$

$x = 1, y = -(1)^2 + 2(1) + 5 = -1 + 2 + 5 = 6$

$x = 2, y = -(2)^2 + 2(2) + 5 = -4 + 4 + 5 = 5$

$x = 4, y = (4)^2 - 8(4) + 16 = 16 - 32 + 16 = 0$

$x = 5, y = (5)^2 - 8(5) + 16 = 25 - 40 + 16 = 1$

It follows that the maximum is $y = 6$ occurring at $x = 1$, and the minimum is $y = 0$ occurring at $x = 4$. (See Figure 1)

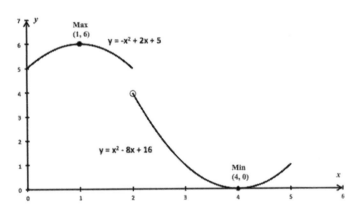

Figure 1

25. From Figure 5.4, relative minima are 5 at t = 0, 3 at $t = 2$, 2 at $t = 6$, and 3.5 at $t = 9$

27. No; No

29. First, find the derivative of the function $y(x) = x^3 - 21x^2 + 120x - 100$. We have:

$y'(x) = 3x^{3-1} - 21(2x^{2-1}) + 120 - 0 = 3x^2 - 42x + 120.$

To locate all values of x for which the derivative is 0, we set the derivative to zero and solve for x. We have:

$$3x^2 - 42x + 120 = 0$$

$$3(x^2 - 14x + 40) = 0$$

$$\frac{3(x^2 - 14x + 40)}{3} = \frac{0}{3}$$

$$x^2 - 14x + 40 = 0$$

$$(x - 10)(x - 4) = 0$$

$$\begin{array}{ccc} x - 10 = 0 & or & x - 4 = 0 \\ +10 \quad +10 & & +4 \quad +4 \\ x = 10 & & x = 4 \end{array}$$

Next, find the second derivative of the function $y(x) = x^3 - 21x^2 + 120x - 100$. We have:

$$y''(x) = \frac{d}{dx}\left(3x^2 - 42x + 120\right) = 3\left(2x^{2-1}\right) - 42 + 0 = 6x - 42.$$

For $x = 4$, $y''(4) = 6(4) - 42 = 24 - 42 = -18 < 0$. Therefore, a relative maximum occurs at $x = 4$. To find the relative maximum, substitute $x = 4$ into the function $y(x) = x^3 - 21x^2 + 120x - 100$. We have:

relative maximum: $y(4) = (4)^3 - 21(4)^2 + 120(4) - 100 = 108$

For $x = 10$, $y''(10) = 6(10) - 42 = 60 - 42 = 18 > 0$. Therefore, a relative minimum occurs at $x = 10$. To find the relative minimum, substitute $x = 10$ into the function $y(x) = x^3 - 21x^2 + 120x - 100$. We have:

relative minimum: $y(10) = (10)^3 - 21(10)^2 + 120(10) - 100 = 0$

Section 5.3: Maximizing Sales Profit

1. (a) Profit = Revenue – Total Cost

$$P(x) = 200x - \left(5{,}000 + 20x + \frac{1}{2}x^2\right)$$

$$= 200x - 5{,}000 - 20x - \frac{1}{2}x^2$$

$$= -\frac{1}{2}x^2 + 180x - 5{,}000$$

(b) Domain: $0 \le x \le 300$

(c) Differentiating the given function, we have:

$$P'(x) = -\frac{1}{2}\left(2x^{2-1}\right) + 180 - 0 = -\frac{2}{2}x + 180 = -x + 180.$$

To locate all values of x for which the derivative is 0, we set the derivative to zero and solve for x. We have:

$$-x + 180 = 0$$

$$\underline{-180 \quad -180}$$

$$-x = -180$$

$$x = 180$$

The derivative exists everywhere, and the endpoints are $x = 0$ and $x = 300$. Evaluating the function at $x = 0$, $x = 180$, and $x = 300$, we have:

$x = 0$, $P(0) = -\frac{1}{2}(0)^2 + 180(0) - 5{,}000 = -\$5{,}000$

$x = 180$, $P(180) = -\frac{1}{2}(180)^2 + 180(180) - 5{,}000 = \$11{,}200$

$x = 300$, $P(300) = -\frac{1}{2}(300)^2 + 180(300) - 5{,}000 = \$4{,}000$

If the manufacturer sells 180 units per week, its profit is $11,200.

3. (a) Profit = Revenue – Total Cost

$$P(x) = 10x - \left(\frac{1}{4{,}000}x^2 - 5x + 50{,}000\right) = 10x - \frac{1}{4{,}000} + 5x - 50{,}000$$

$$= -\frac{1}{4{,}000}x^2 + 15x - 50{,}000$$

(b) Domain: $0 \le x \le 50{,}000$.

(c) Differentiating the given function, we have:

$$P'(x) = -\frac{1}{4{,}000}(2x^{2-1}) + 15 - 0 = -\frac{2}{4{,}000}x + 15 = -\frac{1}{2{,}000}x + 15.$$

To locate all values of x for which the derivative is 0, we set the derivative to zero and solve for x.

$$-\frac{1}{2{,}000}x + 15 = 0 \qquad\qquad \frac{1}{2{,}000}x = 15$$

$$\underline{-15 \quad -15} \qquad\qquad 2{,}000 \cdot \frac{1}{2{,}000}x = 15(2{,}000)$$

$$-\frac{1}{2{,}000}x = -15 \qquad\qquad \frac{2000}{2{,}000}x = 30{,}000$$

$$\left(-\frac{1}{2{,}000}x\right) = -(-15) \qquad\qquad x = 30{,}000 \text{ units}$$

The derivative exists everywhere, and the endpoints are $x = 0$ and $x = 50{,}000$. Evaluating the function at $x = 0$, $x = 30{,}000$, and $x = 50{,}000$, we have:

$x = 0$, $P(0) = -\frac{1}{4{,}000}(0)^2 + 15(0) - 50{,}000 = 0 + 0 - 50{,}000 = -\$50{,}000$

$x = 30{,}0000$, $P(30{,}000) = -\frac{1}{4{,}000}(30{,}000)^2 + 15(30{,}000) - 50{,}000 = \$175{,}000$

$$x = 50,000, P(50,000) = -\frac{1}{4,000}(50,000)^2 + 15(50,000) - 50,000 = \$75,000$$

If the company sells 30,000 units, its profit is $175,000.

5. Differentiating the cost function, we have:

$$C'(x) = \frac{1}{4,000}(2x^{2-1}) - 5 + 0 = \frac{2}{4,000}x - 5 = \frac{1}{2,000}x - 5.$$

To locate all values of x for which the derivative is 0, we set the derivative to zero and solve for x.

$$\frac{1}{2,000}x - 5 = 0$$

$$\frac{1}{2,000}x = 5$$

$$2,000 \cdot \frac{1}{2,000}x = 5(2,000)$$

$$\frac{2000}{2,000}x = 10,000$$

$$x = 10,000 \text{ units}$$

The derivative exists everywhere, and the endpoints are $x = 0$ and $x = 50,000$. Evaluating the function at $x = 10,000$, and $x = 50,000$, we have:

$$x = 0, C(0) = \frac{(0)^2}{4,000} - 5(0) + 50,000 = 0 - 5 + 50,000 = \$50,000$$

$$x = 10,000, C(10,000) = \frac{(10,000)^2}{4,000} - 5(10,000) + 50,000$$

$$= 25,000 - 50,000 + 50,000 = \$25,000$$

$$x = 50,000, C(50,000) = \frac{(50,000)^2}{4,000} - 5(50,000) + 50,000$$

$$= 625,000 - 250,000 + 50,000 = \$425,000$$

To minimize costs, the company should sell 10,000 units.

7. (a) $R(x) = (500 - 2x)x = 500x - 2x^2$

(b) Profit = Revenue − Cost

$$P(x) = 500x - 2x^2 - (300x + 2,000) = 500x - 2x^2 - 300x - 2,000$$
$$= -2x^2 + 200x - 2,000$$

(c) Domain: $0 \leq x \leq 40$

(d) Differentiating the profit function, we have:

$$P'(x) = -2(2x^{2-1}) + 200 - 0 = -4x + 200$$

To locate all values of x for which the derivative is 0, we set the derivative to zero and solve for x.

$$-4x + 200 = 0$$
$$-200 \quad -200$$
$$-4x = -200$$
$$\frac{-4x}{-4} = \frac{-200}{-4}$$

$x = 50$ refrigerators

Because $x = 50$ is outside our domain and is not an allowable point for this problem, we disregard it. The derivative exists everywhere, and the endpoints are $x = 0$ and $x = 40$. Evaluating the function at $x = 0$ and $x = 40$, we have:

$$x = 0, \ P(0) = -2(0)^2 + 200(0) - 2{,}000 = -\$2{,}000$$

$$x = 40, P(40) = -2(40)^2 + 200(40) - 2{,}000 = -3{,}200 + 8{,}000 - 2{,}000 = \$2{,}800$$

If the manufacturer produced 40 refrigerators, its profit is \$2,800.

9. Marginal revenue is the derivative of the revenue.

(a) $MR = R'(x) = 15$.

(b) $MR = R'(x) = 200 - \frac{1}{4}(2x^{2-1}) = 200 - \frac{2}{4}x = 200 - \frac{1}{2}x$

(c) $MR = R'(x) = 2.25 - 0.000025(2x^{2-1}) = 2.25 - 0.00005x$

11. Marginal cost is the derivative of cost:

(a) $MC = C'(x) = \frac{1}{5{,}000}(2x^{2-1}) + 8 + 0 = \frac{2}{5{,}000}x + 8 = \frac{1}{2{,}500}x + 8$

(b) $MC = C'(x) = 50 + 0 = 50$

(c) $MC = C'(x) = 0 + 0.25 = 0.25$

13. Set $R'(x) = C'(x)$, where $R(x) = 200x$ and $C(x) = 5{,}000 + 20x + \frac{1}{2}x^2$, and solve for x. We have:

$$200 = 20 + x$$
$$-20 \quad -20$$
$$180 = x$$

Because $x = 180$ is outside our domain ($0 \leq x \leq 150$) and is not an allowable point for this problem, we disregard it. The derivative exists everywhere, and the endpoints are $x = 0$ and $x = 150$. Evaluating the function $P(x) = -\frac{1}{2}x^2 + 180x - 5{,}000$ at $x = 0$ and $x = 150$, we have:

$x = 0, P(0) = -\frac{1}{2}(0)^2 + 180(0) - 5{,}000 = -\$5{,}000$

$x = 150, P(150) = -\frac{1}{2}(150)^2 + 180(150) - 5{,}000 = \$10{,}750$

If the manufacturer produced 150 televisions, its profit will be $10,750.

15. $R'(x) = C'(x)$

$\quad 500 - 2(2x^{2-1}) = 300$

$\quad 500 - 4x = 300$

$\quad -500 \qquad -500$

$\quad\quad -4x = -200$

$\quad \dfrac{-4x}{-4} = \dfrac{-200}{-4}$

$\quad\quad x = 50$ Refrigerators

The derivative exists everywhere, and the endpoints are $x = 0$, $x = 50$ and $x = 100$. Evaluating the function at $x = 0$, $x = 50$, and $x = 100$, we have:

$x = 0, \; P(0) = -2(0)^2 + 200(0) - 2{,}000 = -\$2{,}000$

$x = 50, \; P(50) = -2(50)^2 + 200(50) - 2{,}000 = -5{,}000 + 10{,}000 - 2{,}000 = \$3{,}000$

$x = 100, \; P(100) = -2(100)^2 + 200(100) - 2{,}000 = -20{,}000 + 20{,}000 - 2{,}000$

$\qquad\qquad\qquad = -\$2{,}000$

The manufacturer should produce 50 refrigerators per week to have a maximum profit of $3,000.

Section 5.4: Minimizing Inventory Costs

1. $m = \$10, k = \$3$, and $D = 540$. The optimum order size (EOQ) $= x = \sqrt{\dfrac{2mD}{k}}$.

$EOQ = x = \sqrt{\dfrac{2(10)(540)}{3}} = \sqrt{\dfrac{10{,}800}{3}} = \sqrt{3{,}600} = 60$ items

3. Before we compute the optimum order size(EOQ), we must convert every parameter to yearly value. Using dimensional analysis, we have:

$k = \dfrac{\$2}{month} \cdot \dfrac{12\ months}{1\ year} = \$24$ per year.

The optimum order size (EOQ) $= x = \sqrt{\dfrac{2mD}{k}} = \sqrt{\dfrac{2(4.80)(1000)}{24}} = \sqrt{\dfrac{9,600}{24}} = \sqrt{400} = 20$

5. (a) $m = \$9.60, k = \$1.92,$ and $D = 1,000.$

The optimum order size (EOQ) $= \sqrt{\dfrac{2mD}{k}} = \sqrt{\dfrac{2(9.60)(1000)}{1.92}} = \sqrt{\dfrac{19,200}{1.92}}$

$$= \sqrt{10,000} = 100 \text{ units}$$

(b) The number of orders placed in a year: $N = \dfrac{D}{x} = \dfrac{1000}{100} = 10$ orders per year.

7. (a) 800

(b) $N = \dfrac{D}{x} = \dfrac{2,400}{800} = 3$ orders per year.

(c) $D = N \cdot x = 3 \cdot 800 = 2,400$ appliances

9.

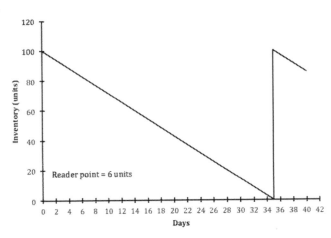

11. Differentiating $TC(x) = mDx^{-1} + \dfrac{k}{2}x$, for $1 \le x \le D$, we have:

$$TC'(x) = mD(-1x^{-1-1}) + \frac{k}{2} = -mDx^{-2} + \frac{k}{2}.$$

To locate all values of x for which the derivative is 0, we set the derivative to zero and solve for x. We have:

$$-mDx^{-2} + \frac{k}{2} = 0 \qquad\qquad 2 \cdot mD = \frac{kx^2}{2} \cdot 2$$

$$\frac{-mD}{x^2} + \frac{k}{2} = 0 \qquad\qquad 2mD = kx^2$$

$$\frac{-mD}{x^2} = -\frac{k}{2} \qquad\qquad \frac{2mD}{k} = \frac{kx^2}{k}$$

$$x^2 \cdot \frac{-mD}{x^2} = -\frac{k}{2} \cdot x^2 \qquad\qquad \frac{2mD}{k} = x^2$$

$$-mD = -\frac{kx^2}{2} \qquad\qquad x^2 = \frac{2mD}{k}$$

$$-(-mD) = -\left(-\frac{kx^2}{2}\right) \qquad\qquad x = \pm\sqrt{\frac{2mD}{k}}$$

Since the value of x is positive, $x = -\sqrt{\frac{2mD}{k}}$ is outside our domain and is not an

allowable point for this problem, we disregard it. The only solution is $x = \sqrt{\frac{2mD}{k}}$. Now,

we find the second derivative for the function $TC(x) = mDx^{-1} + \frac{k}{2}x$:

$$TC''(x) = \frac{d}{dx}\left(-mDx^{-2} + \frac{k}{2}\right) = -mD(-2x^{-2-1}) + 0 = 2mDx^{-3} = \frac{2mD}{x^3} > 0 \text{ for}$$

every x in [1, D]. For $x = \sqrt{\frac{2mD}{k}}$, $TC''\left(\sqrt{\frac{2mD}{k}}\right) = \frac{2mD}{\left(\sqrt{\frac{2mD}{k}}\right)^3}$. We see that $\dfrac{2mD}{\left(\sqrt{\frac{2mD}{k}}\right)^3} > 0$

because $2mD > 0$, $\sqrt{\frac{2mD}{k}} > 0$, and $\left(\sqrt{\frac{2mD}{k}}\right)^3 > 0$. Hence, $\dfrac{2mD}{\left(\sqrt{\frac{2mD}{k}}\right)^3} > 0$.

Therefore, by the second derivative test, $TC(x)$ achieves a relative minimum at $x = \sqrt{\frac{2mD}{k}}$.

Section 5.5: Econometrics

1. $\dfrac{dT}{dB} = \dfrac{1}{1-m} = \dfrac{1}{1-0.6} = \dfrac{1}{0.4} = 2.5 = \dfrac{2.5}{1}$. That is, T increases 2.5 units with every one-unit

change in B. A \$25 million change in B results in a theoretical change of $2.5 \cdot \$25\ million = \$62.5\ million$ in T.

3. With $T = C + B$ and $C = mT + C_0$, where C_0 is fixed, we can write a T as
$T = mT + C_0 + B$. Solving the resulting equation for T, we have:

$$T = mT + C_0 + B$$

$$-mT \quad -mT$$

$$T - mT = B + C_0$$

$$T(1 - m) = B + C_0$$

$$\frac{T(1-m)}{(1-m)} = \frac{B+C_0}{(1-m)}$$

$$T = \frac{B+C_0}{(1-m)} = \frac{B}{1-m} + \frac{C_0}{1-m} = \left(\frac{1}{1-m}\right)B + \frac{C_0}{1-m}$$

$$\frac{dT}{dB} = \frac{1}{1-m} + 0 = \frac{1}{1-m}$$

$$\frac{dT}{dB} = \frac{1}{1-m} = \frac{1}{1-0.6} = \frac{1}{0.4} = 2.5 = \frac{2.5}{1}.$$ That is, T increases 2.5 units with every

one-unit change in B. A \$25 million change in B results in a theoretical change of

$$2.5 \cdot \$25\ million = \$62.5\ million\ \text{in}\ T.$$

5. \$2,383.36 increase

Chapter 6 Curve Fitting and Trend Lines

Section 6.1: Constant Curve Fit

1. $y = \dfrac{12+13+9+8+11+10+9+13+8+10}{10} = \dfrac{103}{10} = 10.3$

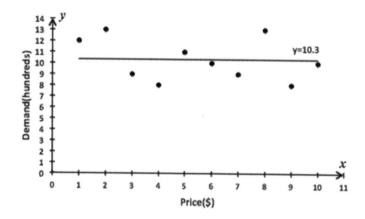

3. $y = \dfrac{28+29+32+27+26+31+28+27+30}{9} = \dfrac{258}{9} = 28.7$

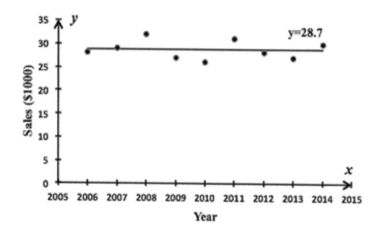

5. An increase does not seem advisable, as sales appear to decrease as advertising is increased. (In Section 6.2, the average rate of change of sales with respect to advertising can be determined, which will show that sales do, in fact, decrease with an increase in advertising—see the solution to Exercise 1 in Section 6.2.)

Section 6.2: Linear Least-Squares Trend Lines

1. (Exercise 5, Page 141)

TABLE 6.4

Year	2006	2007	2008	2009	2010	2011	2012	2013	2014
Advertising ($1,000)	140	150	160	170	180	160	160	170	170
Sales	28	29	32	26	26	27	28	27	30

To find the least-squares straight line ($y = mx + b$) for the data in TABLE 6.4, we need to solve the system of equations:

(1) $bN + m\sum_{i=1}^{N} x_i = \sum_{i=1}^{N} y_i$

(2) $b\sum_{i=1}^{N} x_i + m\sum_{i=1}^{N}(x_i)^2 = \sum_{i=1}^{N}(x_i y_i)$

A good procedure for calculating the least-squares straight line is to first construct table for the values in the equations (1) and (2). We have:

x_i	y_i	$(x_i)^2$	$x_i y_i$
140	28	19,600	3,920
150	29	22,500	4,350
160	32	25,600	5,120
170	26	28,900	4,420
180	26	32,400	4,680
160	27	25,600	4,320
160	28	25,600	4,480
170	27	28,900	4,590
170	30	28,900	5,100
$\sum_{i=1}^{9} x_i = 1,460$	$\sum_{i=1}^{9} y_i = 253$	$\sum_{i=1}^{9}(x_i)^2 = 238,000$	$\sum_{i=1}^{9}(x_i y_i) = 40,980$

Equations (1) and (2) become:

(1) $9b + 1460m = 253$
(2) $1460b + 238,000m = 40,980$

Using the Elimination Method, we will remove b by multiplying equation (1) by $-1,460$ and equation (2) by 9. We have:

(1) $-1,460(9b + 1,460m = 253)$ $\leftrightarrow$ $-13,140b - 2,131,600m = -369,380$
(2) $9(1,460b + 238,000m = 40,980)$ $\leftrightarrow$ $13,140b + 2,142,000m = 368,820$

Add equations (1) and (2). The resulting equation is $10,400m = -560$. Solving the equation for m, we have $m = \frac{-560}{10,400} = -0.0538$. To find b, we substitute $m = -0.0538$ into either equation (1) or (2). Either equations will result in the same b. So, let's choose equation (1). We have:

$$9b + 1460m = 253$$

$$9b + 1460(-0.0538) = 253$$

$$9b - 78.548 = 253$$

$$+78.548 \quad + 78.548$$

$$9b = 331.548$$

$$\frac{9b}{9} = \frac{331.548}{9}$$

$$b = 36.839$$

Therefore, the least-squares straight line is $y = -0.0538x + 36.839$, where y represents Sales and x represents Advertising Budget. Because sales go down (The slope $m = -0.0538$ is negative) as advertising increased, it does not make sense to increase the advertising budget (See Figure 1)

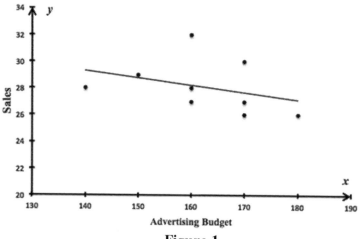

Figure 1

3. (a)

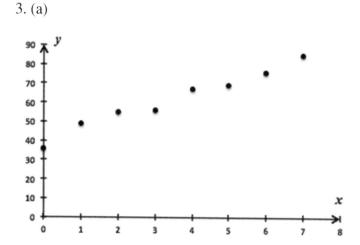

Yes. A straight-line approximation for the trend seems quite reasonable. We see that as the value of x increases, y also increases.

(b)

x	0	1	2	3	4	5	6	7
y	36	49	55	56	67	69	76	85

To find the least-squares straight line ($y = mx + b$) for the data, we need to solve the system of equations:

(1) $bN + m\sum_{i=1}^{N} x_i = \sum_{i=1}^{N} y_i$

(2) $b\sum_{i=1}^{N} x_i + m\sum_{i=1}^{N} (x_i)^2 = \sum_{i=1}^{N} (x_i y_i)$

A good procedure for calculating the least-squares straight line is to first construct table for the values in the equations (1) and (2).

We have:

x_i	y_i	$(x_i)^2$	$x_i y_i$
0	36	0	0
1	49	1	49
2	55	4	110
3	56	9	168
4	67	16	268
5	69	25	345
6	76	36	456
7	85	49	595
$\sum_{i=1}^{8} x_i = 28$	$\sum_{i=1}^{8} y_i = 493$	$\sum_{i=1}^{8} (x_i)^2 = 140$	$\sum_{i=1}^{8} (x_i y_i) = 1{,}991$

Equations (1) and (2) become:

(3) $8b + 28m = 493$
(4) $28b + 140m = 1{,}991$

Using the Elimination Method, we will remove b by multiplying equation (1) by -28 and equation (2) by 8. We have:

(1) $-28(8b + 28m = 493)$ $\leftrightarrow$ $-224b - 784m = -13{,}804$
(2) $8(28b + 140m = 1{,}991)$ $\leftrightarrow$ $224b + 1{,}120m = 15{,}928$

Add equations (1) and (2). The resulting equation is $336m = 2{,}124$. Solving the equation for m, we have $m = \frac{2{,}124}{336} = 6.321$. To find b, we substitute $m = 6.321$ into either equation (1) or (2). Either equation will result with the same b. So, let's choose equation (1). We have:

$8b + 28m = 493$

$8b + 28(6.321) = 493$

$8b + 176.988 = 493$

$\quad -176.988 \quad -176.988$

$8b = 316.012$

$$\frac{8b}{8} = \frac{316.012}{8}$$

$b = 39.502$

Therefore, the least-squares straight line is $y = 6.321x + 39.502$.

(c)

Given Data		Evaluated
x	y	$y = 6.321x + 39.502$
0	36	$6.321(0) + 39.502 = 39.502$
1	49	$6.321(1) + 39.502 = 45.823$
2	55	$6.321(2) + 39.502 = 52.144$
3	56	$6.321(3) + 39.502 = 58.465$
4	67	$6.321(4) + 39.502 = 64.786$
5	69	$6.321(5) + 39.502 = 71.107$
6	76	$6.321(6) + 39.502 = 77.428$
7	85	$6.321(7) + 39.502 = 83.749$

$e(0) = 36 - 39.502 = -3.502$
$e(1) = 49 - 45.823 = 3.177$
$e(2) = 55 - 52.144 = 2.856$
$e(3) = 56 - 58.465 = -2.465$
$e(4) = 67 - 64.786 = 2.214$
$e(5) = 69 - 71.107 = -2.107$
$e(6) = 76 - 77.428 = -1.428$
$e(7) = 85 - 83.749 = 1.251$

The least-squares error:

$E = [e(0)]^2 + [e(1)]^2 + [e(2)]^2 + [e(3)]^2 + [e(4)]^2 + [e(5)]^2 + [e(6)]^2 + [e(7)]^2$

$= (-3.502)^2 + (3.177)^2 + (2.856)^2 + (-2.465)^2 + (2.214)^2 + (-2.107)^2 + (-1.428)^2 + (1.251)^2$

$= 49.536$

(d)

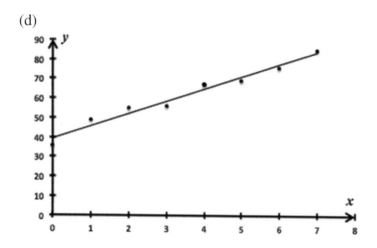

5. (a) Let 1 represent the year 2007, 2 for 2008, 3 for 2009, etc. TABLE 6.14 becomes:

Year	1	2	3	4	5	6	7
Sales(thousands)	15	18	16	20	18	22	19

To find the least-squares straight line ($y = mx + b$) for the data, we need to solve the system of equations:

$$(1) \quad bN + m\sum_{i=1}^{N} x_i = \sum_{i=1}^{N} y_i$$

$$(2) \quad b\sum_{i=1}^{N} x_i + m\sum_{i=1}^{N}(x_i)^2 = \sum_{i=1}^{N}(x_i y_i)$$

A good procedure for calculating the least-squares straight line is to first construct table for the values in the equations (1) and (2).

We have:

x_i	y_i	$(x_i)^2$	$x_i y_i$
1	15	1	15
2	18	4	36
3	16	9	48
4	20	16	80
5	18	25	90
6	22	36	132
7	19	49	133
$\sum_{i=1}^{7} x_i = 28$	$\sum_{i=1}^{7} y_i = 128$	$\sum_{i=1}^{7}(x_i)^2 = 140$	$\sum_{i=1}^{7}(x_i y_i) = 534$

Equations (1) and (2) become:

(1) $7b + 28m = 128$
(2) $28b + 140m = 534$

Using the Elimination Method, we will remove b by multiplying equation (1) by -28 and equation (2) by 7. We have:

(1) $-28(7b + 28m = 128) \leftrightarrow -196b - 784m = -3,584$
(2) $7(28b + 140m = 534) \leftrightarrow \quad 196b + 980m = 3,738$

Add equations (1) and (2). The resulting equation is $196m = 154$. Solving the equation for m, we have: $m = \frac{154}{195} = 0.786$. To find b, we substitute $m = 0.786$ into either equation (1) or (2). Either equation will result with the same b. So, let's choose equation (1). We have:

$$7b + 28m = 128$$
$$7b + 28(0.786) = 128$$
$$7b + 22.008 = 128$$
$$-22.008 \quad -22.008$$
$$7b = 105.992$$
$$\frac{7b}{7} = \frac{105.992}{7}$$
$$b = 15.142$$

Therefore, the least-squares straight line is $y = 0.786x + 15.142$, where y represents Sales and x represents year.

(b) The year 2011 is represented by $x = 5$.

Therefore, Sales = $y = 0.786(5) + 15.142 = \$19.072$ thousands or $19,072.

(c) The year 2018 is represented by $x = 12$.

Therefore, Sales = $y = 0.786(12) + 15.142 = 24.574$ thousands or $24,574.

7.

TABLE 6.16

Rain (inches)	2.0	2.2	2.3	3.2	3.8	4.9	5.6
Yield (bushels)	25	25	30	30	40	50	50

To find the least-squares straight line ($y = mx + b$) for the data, we need to solve the system of equations:

$$(1) \quad bN + m\sum_{i=1}^{N} x_i = \sum_{i=1}^{N} y_i$$

$$(2) \quad b\sum_{i=1}^{N} x_i + m\sum_{i=1}^{N} (x_i)^2 = \sum_{i=1}^{N} (x_i y_i)$$

A good procedure for calculating the least-squares straight line is to first construct table for the values in the equations (1) and (2). We have:

x_i	y_i	$(x_i)^2$	$x_i y_i$
2.0	25	4	50
2.2	25	4.84	55
2.3	30	5.29	69
3.2	30	10.24	96
3.8	40	14.44	152
4.9	50	24.01	245
5.6	50	31.36	280
$\sum_{i=1}^{7} x_i = 24$	$\sum_{i=1}^{7} y_i = 250$	$\sum_{i=1}^{7} (x_i)^2 = 94.18$	$\sum_{i=1}^{7} (x_i y_i) = 947$

Equations (1) and (2) become:

(1) $7b + 24m = 250$
(2) $24b + 94.18m = 947$

Using the Elimination Method, we will remove b by multiplying equation (1) by -24 and equation (2) by 7. We have:

(1) $-24(7b + 24m = 250)$ $\leftrightarrow$ $-168b - 576m = -6,000$
(2) $7(24b + 94.18m = 947)$ $\leftrightarrow$ $168b + 659.26m = 6,629$

Add equations (1) and (2). The resulting equation is $83.26m = 629$. Solving the equation for m, we have $m = \frac{629}{83.26} = 7.555$. To find b, we substitute $m = 7.5546$ into either equation (1) or (2). Either equation will result with the same b. So, let's choose equation (1).

We have:

$7b + 24m = 250$

$7b + 24(7.5546) = 250$

$7b + 181.3104 = 250$

$\quad\quad -181.3104 \quad -181.3104$

$7b = 68.6896$

$\frac{7b}{7} = \frac{68.6896}{7}$

$b = 9.8128$

Therefore, the least-squares straight line is $y = 7.5546x + 9.8128$, where y represent Yield and x represent inches of rain.

For $x = 3.5$, Yield $= y = 7.5546(3.5) + 9.8128 = 36.2539$.

Section 6.3: Quadratic and Exponential Trend Lines

1. **By hand calculations:**

TABLE 6.22

x	0	1	2	3	4
y	10	11	15	16	23

Algebraically

To find the least-squares quadratic trend line ($y = ax^2 + bx + c$) for the data, we need to solve the system of equations:

(1) $\quad cN + b\sum_{i=1}^{N} x_i + a\sum_{i=1}^{N}(x_i)^2 = \sum_{i=1}^{N} y_i$

(2) $\quad c\sum_{i=1}^{N} x_i + b\sum_{i=1}^{N}(x_i)^2 + a\sum_{i=1}^{N}(x_i)^3 = \sum_{i=1}^{N}(x_i y_i)$

(3) $\quad c\sum_{i=1}^{N}(x_i)^2 + b\sum_{i=1}^{N}(x_i)^3 + a\sum_{i=1}^{N}(x_i)^4 = \sum_{i=1}^{N}(x_i)^2 y_i$

A good procedure for calculating the least-squares quadratic trend line is to first construct table for the values in the equations (1), (2), and (3). We have:

x_i	y_i	$(x_i)^2$	$(x_i)^3$	$(x_i)^4$	$x_i y_i$	$(x_i)^2 y_i$
0	10	0	0	0	0	0
1	11	1	1	1	11	11
2	15	4	8	16	30	60
3	16	9	27	81	48	144
4	23	16	64	256	92	368
SUM=10	SUM=75	SUM=30	SUM=100	SUM=354	SUM=181	SUM=583

Equations (1), (2), and (3) become:

(1) $5c + 10b + 30a = 75$

(2) $10c + 30b + 100a = 181$

(3) $30c + 100b + 354a = 583$

To solve a system of three equations with three variables, the objective is to reduce it to a system of two equations with two variables by eliminating one variable of your choosing. Then, reduce the system of two equations with two variables to one equation with one variable. After that, back substitute to find the other two missing variables.

STEP 1: Using the Additive Method (Elimination), choose to remove c by combining any two equations from the three. This in turn will create a system of two equations with two variables. Let's combine equations (1) and (2) and (1) and (3).
Eliminate c by multiplying equation (1) by -10 and equation (2) by 5.

(1) $5c + 10b + 30a = 75 \qquad \leftrightarrow \quad -10(5c + 10b + 30a = 75)$
(2) $10c + 30b + 100a = 181 \leftrightarrow \quad 5(10c + 30b + 100a = 181)$

$\leftrightarrow -50c - 100b - 300a = -750$
$\leftrightarrow \quad 50c + 150b + 500a = 905$

Add equations (1) and (2). The resulting equation is $50b + 200a = 155$. Let's call this new equation (A).

STEP 2: Repeat this procedure for equations (1) and (3). Eliminate c by multiplying equation (1) by -30 and equation (3) by 5.

(1) $5c + 10b + 30a = 75$ $\quad\leftrightarrow\quad -30(5c + 10b + 30a = 75)$
(3) $30c + 100b + 354a = 583$ $\leftrightarrow\quad 5(30c + 100b + 354a = 583)$

$\leftrightarrow -150c - 300b - 900a = -2{,}250$
$\leftrightarrow \quad 150c + 500b + 1{,}770a = 2{,}915$

Add equations (1) and (3). The resulting equation is $200b + 870a = 665$. Let's call this new equation (B).

STEP 3: We now have a system of two equations with two variables.

(A) $\quad 50b + 200a = 155$
(B) $\quad 200b + 870a = 665$

Using the Addition Method, reduce this system of two equations with two variables to one equation with one variable. Once again, choose either b or a to eliminate. Let's choose to eliminate b by multiplying equation (A) by -200 and equation (B) by 50.

(A) $\quad 50b + 200a = 155$ $\;\leftrightarrow\; -200(50b + 200a = 155)$
(B) $200b + 870a = 655$ $\;\leftrightarrow\;\quad 50(200b + 870a = 665)$

$\leftrightarrow -10{,}000b - 40{,}000a = -31{,}000$
$\leftrightarrow \quad 10{,}000b + 43{,}500a = \quad 33{,}250$

Add equations (A) and (B). The resulting equation is $3{,}500a = 2{,}250$. Solving the equation for a, we have $a = \frac{2{,}250}{3{,}500} = 0.643$. To find b, we substitute $a = 0.643$ into either equation (A) or (B). Either equation will result with the same b. So, let's choose equation (A). We have:

$50b + 200a = 155$

$50b + 200(0.643) = 155$

$50b + 128.60 = 155$
$\quad -128.60 \qquad -128.60$

$50b = 26.40$

$\dfrac{50b}{50} = \dfrac{26.40}{50}$

$b = 0.528$

STEP 4: Lastly, we need to find c by substituting the values for a and b into either equation (1), (2), or (3). The same c will be achieved no matter which equation is used. Let's choose equation (1). We have:

$$5c + 10b + 30a = 7$$

$$5c + 10(0.528) + 30(0.643) = 75$$

$$5c + 5.28 + 19.29 = 75$$

$$5c + 24.57 = 75$$

$$\underline{-24.57 \quad -24.57}$$

$$5c = 50.43$$

$$\frac{5c}{5} = \frac{50.43}{5}$$

$$c = 10.086$$

The least-squares quadratic trend line is $y = 0.643x^2 + 0.528x + 10.086$.

By using Excel, we obtain the following graph and its equation:

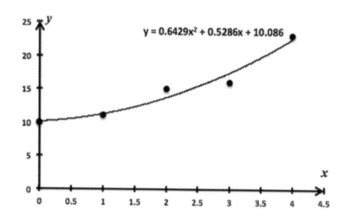

3. **PART 1:** To find the least-squares straight line $(y = mx + b)$ for the data, we need to solve the system of equations:

$$(1) \quad bN + m\sum_{i=1}^{N} x_i = \sum_{i=1}^{N} y_i$$

$$(2) \quad b\sum_{i=1}^{N} x_i + m\sum_{i=1}^{N} (x_i)^2 = \sum_{i=1}^{N} (x_i y_i)$$

A good procedure for calculating the least-squares straight line is to first construct table for the values in the equations (1) and (2). Equations (1) and (2) become:

(1) $5b + 10m = 75$
(2) $10b + 30m = 181$

Using the Elimination Method, we will remove b by multiplying equation (1) by -10 and equation (2) by 5. We have:

(1) $-10(5b + 10m = 75) \leftrightarrow -50b - 100m = -750$
(2) $5(10b + 30m = 181) \leftrightarrow \ 50b + 150m = 905$

Add equations (1) and (2). The resulting equation is $50m = 155$. Solving the equation for m, we have $m = \frac{155}{50} = 3.1$. To find b, we substitute $m = 3.1$ into either equation (1) or (2). Either equation will result with the same b. So, let's choose equation (1). We have:

$5b + 10m = 75$

$5b + 10(3.1) = 75$

$5b + 31 = 75$

$\quad -31 \ \ -31$

$5b = 44$

$\frac{5b}{5} = \frac{44}{5}$

$b = 8.8$

Therefore, the least-squares straight line is $y = 3.1x + 8.8$.

PART 2: Least-squares straight line error.

$x = 0, y = 3.1(0) + 8.8 = 8.8$
$x = 1, y = 3.1(1) + 8.8 = 11.9$
$x = 2, y = 3.1(2) + 8.8 = 15$
$x = 3, y = 3.1(3) + 8.8 = 18.1$
$x = 4, y = 3.1(4) + 8.8 = 21.2$

The least-squares straight line error:

$$E_s = [e(0)]^2 + [e(1)]^2 + [e(2)]^2 + [e(3)]^2 + [e(4)]^2$$

$$= (1.2)^2 + (-.9)^2 + (0)^2 + (-2.1)^2 + (1.8)^2 = 9.9$$

PART 3: The least-squares quadratic trend line error.

$x = 0, y = 0.643(0)^2 + 0.528(0) + 10.086 = 10.086$

$x = 1, y = 0.643(1)^2 + 0.528(1) + 10.086 = 11.257$

$x = 2, y = 0.643(2)^2 + 0.528(2) + 10.086 = 13.714$

$x = 3, y = 0.643(3)^2 + 0.528(3) + 10.086 = 17.457$

$x = 4, y = 0.643(4)^2 + 0.528(4) + 10.086 = 22.486$

The least-squares quadratic trend line error:

$$E_Q = [e(0)]^2 + [e(1)]^2 + [e(2)]^2 + [e(3)]^2 + [e(4)]^2$$

$$= (-.086)^2 + (-.257)^2 + (1.286)^2 + (-1.457)^2 + (.514)^2 = 4.11$$

The least-squares quadratic trend line has smaller error than the least-squares straight line.

PART 4:

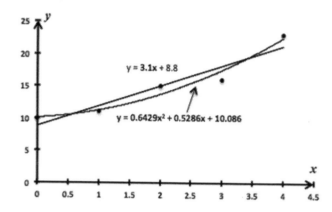

5.

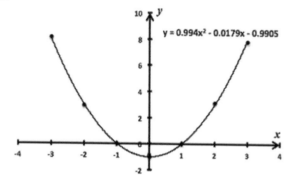

7. (a) Calculating by hand.

x	-1	0	1
y	0	7	10

To find the three simultaneous equations below, we need to find all the sums involved.

(1) $\quad cN + b\sum_{i=1}^{N} x_i + a\sum_{i=1}^{N} (x_i)^2 = \sum_{i=1}^{N} y_i$

(2) $\quad c\sum_{i=1}^{N} x_i + b\sum_{i=1}^{N} (x_i)^2 + a\sum_{i=1}^{N} (x_i)^3 = \sum_{i=1}^{N} (x_i y_i)$

(3) $\quad c\sum_{i=1}^{N} (x_i)^2 + b\sum_{i=1}^{N} (x_i)^3 + a\sum_{i=1}^{N} (x_i)^4 = \sum_{i=1}^{N} (x_i)^2 y_i$

Construct a table for the values in the equations (1), (2), and (3). We have:

x_i	y_i	$(x_i)^2$	$(x_i)^3$	$(x_i)^4$	$x_i y_i$	$(x_i)^2 y_i$
-1	0	1	-1	1	0	0
0	7	0	0	0	0	0
1	10	1	1	1	10	10
SUM =0	SUM= 17	SUM = 2	SUM= 0	SUM=2	SUM=10	SUM=10

Equations (1), (2), and (3) become:

(1) $3c + 0b + 2a = 17 \leftrightarrow 3c + 2a = 17$

(2) $0c + 2b + 0a = 10 \leftrightarrow 2b = 10$

(3) $2c + 0b + 2a = 10 \leftrightarrow 2c + 2a = 10$

(b) To solve a system of three equations with three variables, the objective is to reduce it to a system of two equations with two variables by eliminating one variable of your choosing. Then, reduce the system of two equations with two variables to one equation with one variable. After that, back substitute to find the other two missing variables.

Equation (2) can be solved immediately for b. $b = \frac{10}{2} = 5$. We are now left with only with the values of a and c to find. Using equations (1) and (3), we will be able to determine the values.

Using the Additive Method (Elimination), choose to remove c by multiplying equation (1) by -2 and equation (3) by 3. We have:

(1) $3c + 2a = 17 \leftrightarrow -2(3c + 2a = 17) \leftrightarrow -6c - 4a = -34$
(3) $2c + 2a = 10 \leftrightarrow 3(2c + 2a = 10) \leftrightarrow 6c + 6a = 30$

Add equations (1) and (3). The resulting equation is $2a = -4$. Solving for a, we have:

$a = \frac{-4}{2} = -2$. To find c, we substitute $a = -2$ into either equation (1) or (3). Either equation will results with the same b. So, let's choose equation (1). We have:

$3c + 2a = 17$ $3c = 21$

$3c + 2(-2) = 17$ $\frac{3c}{3} = \frac{21}{3}$

$3c - 4 = 17$ $c = 7$

$ +4 \quad +4$

Therefore, $a = -2, b = 5$, and $c = 7$.

9.

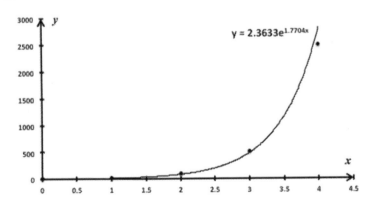

11. (a)

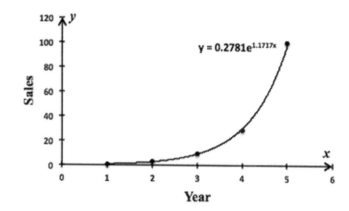

(b) Note: Assuming that 1 represent the year 2001, 2 represent the year 2002, etc.

For $x = 16$, $Sales = y = 0.2781e^{1.1717(16)} = \$38,548,412.71$

Made in the USA
Middletown, DE
02 September 2017